W9-BWG-447

Effective
Discipline

Effective Discipline

Second Edition

DEBORAH DEUTSCH SMITH
DIANE M. RIVERA

ILLUSTRATED BY
JAN CARLEY

pro·ed
8700 Shoal Creek Blvd
Austin, Texas 78757

© 1984, 1993 by PRO-ED, Inc.

All rights reserved. No part of this book
may be reproduced in any form or by any means
without the prior written permission of the publisher.

Printed in the United States of America

Library of Congress Cataloging-in-Publication Data

Smith, Deborah Deutsch.
    Effective discipline / Deborah Deutsch Smith, Diane M. Rivera :
illustrated by Jan Carley.—2nd ed.
      p.   cm.
    Includes bibliographical references and index.
    ISBN 0-89079-579-7
    1. School discipline.   I. Rivera, Diane M.   II. Title.
LA3012.S65   1993
371.5—dc20   92-37935
                                                   CIP

pro·ed
8700 Shoal Creek Blvd
Austin, Texas 78757

2 3 4 5 6 7 8   04 03 02 01 00 99 98

LB
3012
.S65
1993

Contents

Preface

The primary role for educators in preschools through secondary schools is to help individuals learn maximally. Students need to acquire a substantial amount of knowledge, become proficient in basic skills, and develop social skills that will help them become productive members of society. Good instruction cannot be accomplished in chaos. For it to occur, a positive learning environment must be fostered and protected. The learning climate needs to be supportive and open so students can learn, create, discover, explore, and expand their knowledge. Such a conducive educational climate does not exist when disruption is high and when educators spend their time and effort attending to conduct problems. Neither is it fostered when the methods selected to reduce disruption are too punitive or severe.

A positive learning environment can exist in every classroom and school. Disruption can be reduced to a minimum without destroying the delicate learning climate. For this to occur, educators must be informed about the wide variety of interventions that have proven successful through both research and practice. Using this awareness, educators can select the least intrusive or stringent methods first. Because the application of disciplinary interventions must match the disruption, educators need to *intelligently* and *sensitively* evaluate the disruption and the methods used to remediate specific situations. Using a planned approach to discipline will result in the protection of a positive learning environment.

The intent of this book is to provide principals, counselors, and teachers with information about an array of proven techniques that reduce or eliminate school behavior problems. We have included many suggestions about specific intervention procedures that, when used systematically and consistently, should result in a school environment most conducive to the real task of teachers: to educate.

This book has several basic themes. The first is the prevention of school and classroom discipline problems by creating an atmosphere that includes the students in their total school program. School personnel are encouraged to make school exciting and challenging so that disruption is less likely to occur. The second theme centers on the notion that discipline and behavioral control are total school concerns. The best school environment is created when the entire faculty and staff are consistent in their application of interventions and consequences. Third, school personnel should use the mildest and simplest form of intervention first. Only after evaluation procedures indicate that a mild intervention is not successful should more drastic procedures be implemented. Therefore, discussion about direct interventions is presented in a hierarchy, with the least intrusive tactics explained early and the more punitive and difficult to manage last.

CONTENTS OF THE BOOK

We designed this book to provide educators with skills that create a positive learning environment that is free from serious disruptions. Our goals are thus ambitious. The major aims of this book are to give all educators the ability to (a) demonstrate an awareness of how deportment problems can be reduced through organized prevention techniques, (b) identify specifically those behaviors that disrupt the learning environment, (c) demonstrate knowledge of a wide variety of intervention tactics, (d) appropriately match interventions with behavioral infractions by using the least intrusive procedures possible and planning for their limitations, and (e) evaluate and communicate the effectiveness of the interventions they employ.

Chapter 1 focuses on ways to lay a solid foundation for effective discipline practices. A philosophy of discipline, schoolwide practices, and teacher practices are highlighted. Chapter 2 centers directly on preventing conduct problems. Chapters 3 and 4 provide many explanations and examples for different intervention strategies, ranging from mild to more serious procedures. Chapter 5 explains how to judge the effectiveness of these procedures. Guidelines for simple documentation and easy communication of the results of these evaluations are provided. The last chapter includes practice activities that should reinforce the concepts presented in the previous sections. For those interested in studying specific topics in greater depth, the appendix includes a suggested reading list of relevant research articles, literature, reviews, and books.

HOW TO USE THIS BOOK

We designed this book for both the practitioner and the college student preparing to become an educator. Its intent is to be practical yet comprehensive. It is written so the material can be easily absorbed by the reader in several sessions. Therefore, many features are included in this book to make the content more understandable and readily incorporated in school settings. For example, the text includes a liberal use of practical examples and illustrations to emphasize important precautions about specific interventions and ways to match them with specific situations, as well as tips for implementing interventions effectively. To help the reader master the content, we provide advance organizers to prepare the reader for each chapter's content, practice opportunities for applying each chapter's content, questions to stimulate individuals or groups to consider or discuss issues more fully, and chapter objectives for readers to review. Also, we include clear definitions of all basic and technical information; two glossaries of interventions (Tables 3.3 and 4.2), which include definitions and applied examples; checklists; and explanations and examples of how to evaluate and document the effectiveness of the interventions selected and implemented. In addition, the reader will find concise summaries at the end of each chapter and a selected reading list in the appendix.

To help the reader master the information presented, the review sessions in the last chapter provide specific exercises and activities designed to encourage better application of the book's content in school settings. The various activities are intended to stimulate thought and discussion. These review sessions supplement each chapter's practice opportunities and should help educators use the techniques for classroom discipline more effectively.

This book is planned to be useful to either individuals or groups. Individuals will find the review sessions useful for assimilating the information presented in this book. Groups may wish to hold several meetings in which the review activities and exercises are discussed and shared. We suggest that, before groups meet, individuals complete the exercises and activities. In this way, group time can be used for interaction around the principles and concepts presented. Discussions could center on specific disruptive incidents and ways to deal with each most effectively. At the ends of Chapters 3 and 4, lists of common disruptive behaviors are presented. Groups or individuals are encouraged to add their own examples of classroom or schoolwide behavior problems and to brainstorm possible interventions as solutions to the problems.

In short, we organized this book for use as a basic or supplemental text for college students preparing to fill a variety of direct service roles in today's schools (e.g., teachers, counselors, principals, inservice trainers, support personnel). The book is also appropriate for individual professionals who wish to become more fully informed about disciplinary measures that contribute to a positive learning environment. In addition, it is designed for schoolwide inservice training to encourage the adoption of consistent and systematic disciplinary procedures aimed at minimizing conduct problems and enhancing the learning environment.

We have tried to write a practical book that encourages educators to evaluate their own learning environments and those disciplinary measures employed to protect that climate where students are supported to learn and grow. The information presented here is drawn from theory, research, and practice, and is presented in a concise, logical, and easy to assimilate fashion. Our sincere hope is that educators using the information provided in this book will become more sensitive to students' needs, the protection of the delicate educational climate, and the ultimate selection of disciplinary measures that best match inevitable conduct problems.

ACKNOWLEDGMENTS

Throughout the writing of this book, we received unending support and encouragement from many people who are dear to us. In particular, we would like to thank our significant others—Jim, Brian, Steve, and Ryan—whose support made our tasks easier.

We also wish to thank Donald Hammill, Steve Mathews, and Jim Patton for their belief in the project and encouragement through its fruition. This revision is better because of the input of excellent professionals such as Tim Heron and Loretta Serna. We also thank those students and educators who provided valuable input across the years on the first edition. Their comments helped to make the revision more practical and useful.

Lastly, we owe special thanks to two people: Jan Carley, whose cartoons and illustrations add a distinctive element to the text, and Rebecca Fletcher for her assistance with this project.

1
Laying the Foundation

OBJECTIVES

After reading this chapter, you should be able to

1. Discuss factors pertaining to discipline as an issue in education.

2. Describe your philosophy of discipline.

3. Describe ways to promote schoolwide effective discipline.

4. Discuss techniques for teachers to lay the foundation in creating effective discipline practices in the classroom.

5. Participate in "Practice What You've Learned" activities.

Discipline ideas to be discussed in this chapter include

• Philosophy of Discipline
• Schoolwide Practices
Creating a Positive School Climate
Promoting School as a Community
• Teacher Practices
Exerting Influence
Communicating Carefully
Maintaining Consistency
Using Signals
Matching Intervention to Infraction: The Intervention Ladder
Remembering Guiding Principles

DEFINITION

Discipline means that there is order among pupils so learning can take place without competition from unproductive factors. It is a system of rules for conduct and a mechanism for ensuring that conduct codes are followed.

D iscipline is viewed by the American public as *the* major problem facing educators and by those who work in public schools as *very serious* or *fairly serious* (Gallup, 1984, 1986; *The 14th Annual Gallup Poll*, 1982). Many reasons are cited for the lack of discipline in school settings: low teacher salaries, inadequate financial support for public education, large school complexes, insufficient parental support, and a general disregard for authority by the students themselves. Many other reasons for conduct problems in school settings could be listed, such as gang warfare, violent crimes, weapons, and substance abuse. (Although these problems are serious challenges for law enforcers and school administrators, they are beyond the scope of this book. A list of resources on these topics is included in the appendix.) Most of these problems are beyond educators' control and frequently become excuses for why discipline cannot be improved. Armed with these excuses, some educators make no attempt to alter negative situations that they believe are beyond their spheres of influence. This attitude is not constructive: It certainly does not result in the implementation of the positive actions necessary to ameliorate schools' educational climates. Rather, it produces an expectation of discipline problems and a resignation to the deterioration of learning environments.

It is important to remember that the vast majority of school-aged students do not engage in disruptive behavior. Most are well behaved. However, even a small percentage of students can negatively alter the learning envi-

ronment. Regardless of the number of students who disrupt the educational climate, they must not be allowed to impair the learning process for their classmates. Clearly, educators must keep a constant vigil on the learning environment and continually work toward its improvement. School environments can be improved without expensive or elaborate techniques. Discipline problems can be reduced to a minimum if school personnel work as a team to consistently and systematically use educationally sound procedures.

DISCUSSION QUESTIONS

1. What are some societal issues and problems that impact education?
2. Which issues and problems do you think are beyond the control of educators?
3. What services are necessary to help educators deal with some of the societal issues and problems that impact education?
4. What additional training should educators receive to cope more effectively with discipline problems in schools today?
5. How have discipline problems changed in the last decade? How have they remained constant?
6. What is the role of the administrator in disciplining students?
7. What alternatives exist for teachers when administrative support for discipline is lacking?
8. What are the major discipline problems at the preschool, elementary, and secondary levels?

The management of conduct problems is of utmost concern to educators and all those interested in school environments and student achievement. Educators know that for learning and success to occur, a system of order must be in place that establishes parameters for acceptable student behavior and provides consequences for appropriate and inappropriate behavior. This system of order is achieved optimally when educators strive to practice principles of effective discipline. These principles include the following:

1. Create a positive climate.

2. Lay the foundation for a positive learning environment.

3. Focus on prevention.

4. Work as a team with other educators for schoolwide effectiveness.

5. Communicate with other professionals and establish partnerships.

6. Match intervention to infraction.

7. Define target behaviors, implement an intervention, and utilize an evaluation plan frequently to monitor student progress.

By incorporating the principles of effective discipline into their instructional repertoires, educators can foster a climate for success and learning. Then they can spend much of their instructional time on teaching and managing students.

An important initial consideration for developing effective discipline practices is laying the foundation. This involves developing a philosophy of discipline, examining schoolwide practices, and focusing on teacher practices within the classroom.

PHILOSOPHY OF DISCIPLINE

This book is built on the philosophy that conduct that distracts from the learning environment can be managed while a positive atmosphere of growth and learning is maintained. Disciplining students does not have to result in a repressive climate where students behave because they are afraid not to follow conduct codes. Rather, discipline can produce an understanding of the relationship between specific behaviors and their consequences. It can and should result in the social learning and growth of students at the preschool, elementary, and secondary levels.

The primary purpose of the educational system is to teach students those academic and social skills needed by productive members of society. The overriding goal of education is for students to gain the motivation and skills necessary to achieve their individual potential. School personnel must pursue this goal by encouraging each student's mastery of the curriculum. Of course, this is not an easy task, and it seems increasingly more difficult to accomplish each year.

Years ago, it was easier for schools to achieve their purpose. Graduates were expected to be able to read, write, and calculate. Students who were not inclined academically or able to meet the social demands of the structured school setting were not obligated to remain in school. Those students who completed school did so because they and their parents had set the attainment of knowledge and completion of school as an important priority. Today, graduates are still expected to be able to read, write, and calculate, but they also are expected to have mastered more academic subjects, many of which are complex. Schools attempt to prepare students to enter a more demanding and sophisticated world. It is a world which, each decade, requires increasingly more knowledge and skills. In addition to the greater educational demands upon schools, the complexion of the school environment has changed. A set age for both beginning and finishing school is required in all states, and attendance is mandatory. Schools must now accommodate *all* students: those academically and nonacademically inclined, and those who do and do not meet social standards of the school situation. Schools and classrooms are no longer small, a seeming extension of the family. Educators must assist all students in fulfilling their potential in classrooms that may contain over 30 pupils, in schools that range in size from a few hundred to several thousand, and all of this on ever-shrinking budgets. Thus, as the school environment evolves in response to societal factors, it is imperative that a philosophy of discipline be established as the basis for all academic and social learning.

Given the changes in society and the demands placed on educators, it is imperative that each school's staff, as well as the school district as a whole, define its philosophy of discipline. Typically, this philosophy reflects a philosophy of education.

Educators must know the following, both as a school team and individually:

1. What expectations they have for students.

2. What type of learning environment they are willing to promote.

3. How they will respond to appropriate and inappropriate behaviors.

Establishing a philosophy of discipline, then, involves discussions about the following:

1. What motivates behavior.

2. How individuals react toward one another.

3. What constitutes effective problem-solving approaches.

4. How to nurture the development of responsible, independent learners.

DISCUSSION QUESTIONS

1. What are your expectations for students?
2. What are the expectations for students in your school?
3. What is the role of the community in school discipline practices?
4. What motivates students to misbehave?
5. What motivates students to behave?
6. How does the teacher encourage appropriate and inappropriate student behavior?
7. What are some effective problem-solving approaches?
8. What are some ways to teach students to become responsible, independent thinkers and learners?
9. What is your philosophy of education?
10. What is your philosophy of discipline?

SCHOOLWIDE PRACTICES

When students enter school each day, they become members of a school community. The climate of that community includes important dimensions—the cohesiveness of the staff, the instructional leadership, the philosophy of education, the relationship with parents, and the interactions between individuals—that must be considered when establishing effective, positive-oriented discipline practices. The school climate and community are two major themes that need to be examined carefully to enhance effective discipline practices.

Creating a Positive School Climate

Schools are places designed for students to learn and grow both academically and socially. For maximum learning and growth, the educational climate must be positive, supportive, and rich in experiences and opportunities. Furthermore, the learning environment must be free from undue distraction and disruption. This requires discipline.

Of utmost concern to educators is the creation of that delicate environment in which students are free to discover, think creatively, acquire basic knowledge, and develop personally. School is an environment in which too much authoritarianism constricts and too little structure negates the flow of information. To meet the needs of each individual among the many who are at school to learn, educators must keep disruption to a minimum. Only one disruptive student can destroy this delicate balance, and thereby affect the ability of an entire class to gain maximally from the educational situation. Discipline must be achieved so all can profit from the instructional experience. Moreover, the disruptive student must become disciplined to function properly in the learning environment and later in society. However, that discipline should not interfere with the delicate learning environment. It must be positive and constructive, adding to the educational experiences of all students.

Promoting School as a Community

Schools are communities that comprise various and diverse constituencies. The creation and protection of a positive learning environment should be the concern of every group in the school community. When a school functions as a united community, the result is a reduction in the number of occasions requiring discipline measures. Involvement by all groups that belong to the school community can enhance the learning environment. Unfortunately, this involvement is frequently discouraged or not fostered.

LEADERSHIP STYLES. Although there are various ways for groups and individuals to become involved in the learning environment, they are often excluded from active participation. The modus operandi at various schools can differ widely. At some, the principal assumes the sole responsibility for setting the behavioral standards, enforcing the attainment of those standards, and coordinating the disciplinary procedures, while seldom communicating with others. This mode is authoritarian and expects little active involvement from the full range of community members. Other principals adopt a laissez-faire attitude toward the learning environment and discipline by letting individual teachers handle behavior problems as they arise. Some relegate these issues to the school counselor or another administrative representative, whereas others seek various levels of involvement from all members of the school community.

KINDS OF INVOLVEMENT. Although the composition of the school community differs slightly in each setting, generally the community comprises the students, their parents, the educators, and the staff members. Several kinds of involvement in the development and maintenance of a positive learning environment could be offered each group:

- The first kind of involvement centers on the establishment of the code of conduct that represents the standard for acceptable behavior.

- The second relates to the selection of the disciplinary measures used when the code of conduct is violated.

- The third concerns who implements the disciplinary measures.

- The last general level of involvement is awareness, which requires communication about the learning environment, the behavioral standards, and the effectiveness of the interventions implemented.

Different kinds and amounts of involvement can be sought from students, staff members, educators, and parents. The **students** can be actively involved in establishing some of the aspects of the behavioral code. In part, they can participate in determining what disciplinary measures will be taken when the code is violated, and certainly should be an integral part of the communication network. **Staff members**, who are typically excluded from participating in creating and protecting the learning environment, could become more actively involved. For example, the school secretary usually would not apply direct intervention procedures, but could be involved in setting various conduct guidelines and receiving information about how well the imposed interventions are working. The custodians could help set the standards that affect their role in the learning environment, participate in the implementation of measures designed to improve their domain, and be part of the communication network. **Educators** could be involved in a participatory decision-making process in which they have opportunities to provide input about issues and decisions. This creates a sense of ownership whereby people can feel that they have a stake in what happens at their school. Clearly, all staff members and educators have a stake in producing a positive learning environment. Their active participation will benefit the establishment of a positive climate and enhance the probability of its maintenance.

Parents are key members of the educational community. It is important for educators to establish good rapport and partnerships with parents from the start. Parents must feel that they are part of the school community, rather than intruders. The recent rise in parent involvement has been noted by many educators (e.g., Cone, DeLawyer, & Wolfe, 1985; Kroth & Simpson, 1977; Sapon-Shevin, 1982; Smith, 1989). Parents can be a vital part of direct intervention programs designed to reduce or eliminate the conduct problems of their children; however, their role in prevention plans is often overlooked. Parents are rarely contacted by school personnel unless there is a problem at school. The fact that they are not part of the positive communication network is unfortunate, for it leads to hostility and alienation (Kroth, 1985; Rutherford & Edgar, 1979). Just as those individuals who are present at school each day need to become part of a communication network about school activities, so do parents. The achievement of individuals and the school population in general is the concern of all school members. Parents should be informed about the school environment and how it facilitates group and individual achievement.

This communication could be both formal and informal. Examples include

1. Newsletters that provide general information about school

2. Notes about individual student accomplishments (in which every student receives some periodic positive recognition)

3. Telephone calls periodically telling parents good news

4. "Happy Grams" for younger students highlighting something special that happened that day or week

5. Samples of student work so parents have some idea of progress

Notes or telephone conferences could communicate information about positive gains (even when they are slight) made by the student. Such commu-

nication will produce a larger and more supportive community group, which might result in the prevention of conduct problems and the willingness for direct involvement if the need should arise.

DISCUSSION QUESTIONS

1. What type of climate exists in your classroom and school? How is this fostered?

2. How can a school and classroom climate be examined? What are some factors to consider?
3. What are ways to improve the climate?
4. What are some examples of positive discipline practices?
5. How can educators create an environment that provides parameters for appropriate behavior yet allows some freedom for independent thought and activity?
6. What type of leadership style exists at your school?
7. How are different groups involved with decisions at your school?
8. What kinds of involvement occur at your school when decisions about discipline are made?
9. What are ways to establish rapport with parents?
10. How can parents be involved in the school and classroom?
11. What are ways to promote a climate of "school as community"?

TEACHER PRACTICES

The teacher is the most important person in the classroom in terms of setting the climate for the room. The instructor sets the tone for how students are expected to act in the classroom, whether interacting with another person or with instructional materials. The teacher develops and enforces the parameters of appropriate behavior by which students must abide. For the most part, the teacher is the person who institutes consequences, both positive and negative, and who contributes to the development of students who will someday be the adults of our society.

Certain basic practices can assist the teacher in establishing an effective classroom environment that promotes positive discipline and a climate conducive for instructional success. These practices pertain to teacher behaviors, the curriculum and instruction, and classroom management. The focus in this section is on basic teacher practices, which include (a) exerting influence, (b) communicating carefully, (c) maintaining consistency, (d) using signals, (e) matching intervention to infraction, and (f) remembering guiding principles.

Exerting Influence

According to Canter (1986), teachers have basic rights to establish a classroom routine and structure that fits their style, to determine and request appropriate behavior from their pupils, and to ask for help from parents and administrators when they need it. Teachers must exert their influence with pupils by acting more assertively and setting limits for conduct. These limits must be established in a warm and supportive climate where students receive honest feedback about their behavior. Canter provided teachers with guidelines for obtaining a positive level of influence while taking their own wants and feelings more seriously. These guidelines include

1. Using a firm tone of voice.

2. Maintaining eye contact.

3. Using the student's name.

4. Being certain that your gestures (nonverbal behavior) match your verbal message.

5. Touching the student's arm or shoulder when appropriate.

6. Having consequences in mind for student disruption.

7. Following through.

8. Making certain that students know that it is their choice to behave appropriately or not.

The following example helps to illustrate Canter's important points about exerting one's influence:

Ms. Cavalluzzo's students had difficulty changing from one activity to the next. Problems were particularly noticeable when a science project had to be put away each day and the class had to return to an academic task. After analyzing her own behavior during such situations, Ms. Cavalluzzo decided that she was not direct enough in her statements and actions with the students who did not follow her direction. She was not exerting her influence. For these reasons, changing from one activity to another was an unpleasant experience for her and many of her students. Although she was more assertive the next time she requested the class to clean up their science work and begin their next assignment, one child did not make the transition in an acceptable manner. Ms. Cavalluzzo said, "Rick, I want you to clean up and get to work." He replied that he wanted a few more minutes to finish his experiment. She gained eye contact with Rick and restated her request. Rick still indicated that he wanted to finish his work and that it would take only a few minutes. In response, she said, "Rick, no more time. Get to work now or you will have no science time tomorrow. It is your choice." The student then followed her directions, and the transition was accomplished without substantial disruption.

Other factors must be considered for teachers to exert their influence successfully. First, voice level is very important. A trap for a teacher to avoid is raising his or her voice as the noise rises in the classroom. In such situations, teachers end up competing against student noise level to gain attention and control. Instead, many teachers actually lower their voices to a whisper, which often gains student attention and permits teachers to remind students about an excessive level of noise. Also, a calm, firm voice is necessary when disciplining students. Teachers must be careful not to allow themselves to appear out of control.

Second, teacher presence is a very powerful tool for maintaining appropriate behaviors. Teacher presence means that teachers place themselves strategically as a reminder that misbehavior will not be accepted. For example, if a class discussion is occurring and one student seems fidgety, the teacher can stand next to the disrupting student to calm him or her.

Third, teachers can minimize discipline problems through visibility. This implies that teachers should move about the classroom frequently, remaining visible and accessible as much as possible, rather than sitting behind a desk or standing in front of the room. Visibility increases the likelihood of having a good command of the entire classroom situation. Visibility helps teachers anticipate and respond to potentially problematic situations more effectively than responding to situations that have become disruptive.

Fourth, nonverbal cues can be used to send messages to students about their behavior. For example, looking sternly conveys a distinct message about the inappropriateness of a certain behavior. Likewise, crossed arms, finger to lips, looking at the clock, and smiling send nonverbal signals to students that could quickly stop a negative behavior or reinforce a positive one.

Communicating Carefully

The manner in which people communicate with each other affects their interactions. For over a decade, many counselors have advised parents that the way they communicate with children substantially influences their behavior. Advice about effective communication patterns is drawn from Gordon's (1974) work on parent effectiveness training, and comes from a considerable amount of applied efforts with parents and their children. These observations are relevant to educators and their verbal interactions with students.

The basic premise is that the tone of adults' communication with children affects children's responses to adults. Verbal statements may convey different meanings and elicit different responses. Gordon's approach seeks to explain why some communication aimed at reducing or eliminating a bothersome behavior results in increasing or maintaining it. The approach also offers alternative methods of communicating, which should produce better results. In analyses of adults' communications with children, Gordon found that many verbal statements tend to order, direct, command, threaten, admonish, preach, moralize, advise, or mandate solutions. Sometimes teachers' verbal messages ridicule, shame, criticize, or blame students. Such communication outcomes, most likely, do not produce the desired results: Children do not conform to adults' behavioral expectations. Gordon referred to such patterns of verbal interactions as "You-messages." The number of specific You-messages is enormous, but the following examples should illustrate the point: "You stop that." "You sit down." "You should be ashamed of yourself." "You should know better." "You are not behaving appropriately." You-messages can put children on the defensive, cause them to withdraw from adults, or even make them respond in less appropriate ways. A hostile child cannot learn maximally in the educational setting. It is important for students to be open and receptive of the adults in the learning environment. If the teacher–pupil relationship is adversely affected by the way an adult communicates with children, the verbal pattern must be changed.

Gordon offered an alternative method of communicating with students, which he referred to as "I-messages." With these messages, the adult directly or indirectly explains why a situation produced by the adult–child interaction is bothersome at a particular time. The adult offers no solution to the student and, therefore, should provoke less resistance and rebellion. The adult communicates honestly about the effect that the child's behavior has, rather than implying that the child is bad for engaging in the behavior. The following are some examples of I-messages that could be used in classroom situations to prevent major disciplinary problems: "I'm really distracted. It is difficult for me to teach when it is too noisy." "I can't show you how to do this art project well enough because the art table is too messy."

Approaching children by using the I-message should produce some important results in the learning situation. First, the delicate teacher–student relationship could develop into a more mature, honest, and mutually respectful one. This should contribute to an even more positive learning environment in which all members respect and understand each other. Second, students will learn to assume responsibility for their actions and find solutions to inappropriate behavioral situations. Finally, being more careful about the method of communicating information to students about their disruptive behaviors can lead to their prevention and avoid the necessity of direct adult intervention.

Maintaining Consistency

One way to confuse people, regardless of their age, is to place them in situations where procedures are inconsistently scheduled. If a teacher decides to use a reward such as free time, then the students should be allowed to earn it each time the specified conditions are met. If a teacher considers a certain noise level acceptable during a group interchange, that level should be tolerated during all such times. It is unreasonable to expect students to adjust their noise level when environmental cues are subtle and no instructions are given. Within the classroom, teachers need to be consistent in their requirements for appropriate behavior.

The same is true for groups of teachers handling certain situations within a school setting. If a standard is set for conduct during period changes, that standard must be adhered to consistently, regardless of who monitors the corridor. If certain standards or codes of behavior are expected on the grounds before and after school, those standards should be explained to the students and consistently enforced. This requires cooperation and communication among all members of the school community. Everyone must understand what the code of behavior is and what procedures are to be followed when the code is violated.

Because consistency, in itself, reduces the likelihood of conduct problems, it is recommended that all teachers in each of their classes use comparable standards for acceptable behavior and similar methods for ensuring that those standards are met. Although many teachers believe that discipline in their classrooms is their individual concern, that concept is faulty. Schools in which discipline has been achieved commonly have established methods for handling conduct for the entire school. Everyone in the school uses the same kinds of disciplinary tactics consistently. The procedures presented in this book—prevention, intervention, and evaluation—will produce maximal results when they are used consistently by all personnel. This requires group training sessions, group interchanges and discussions, and a standard set of procedures to be implemented when specific behavioral occurrences are observed. Such organized efforts require the support of the school administration. Although one teacher can use the procedures outlined in this text with great success, overall discipline will be best achieved when the procedures represent the actualization of a schoolwide approach to discipline.

Using Signals

A signal is a technique to gain student attention for various reasons, such as quieting students, giving directions, preparing a transition, beginning a lesson, and making announcements. Signals can be audible or visual. Examples of audible signals include ringing a bell, talking softly, counting backward, counting forward, and singing. Visual signals include raising a hand, standing in a specific section of the room, flickering the lights, and crossing arms. Regardless of the teacher's selected signal, the message to the students is to quiet down and listen.

Signals must be taught. First, the teacher presents the rationale for the signal, that is, the need to gain student attention for a specific reason. Second, a signal is selected that is age appropriate. For example, singing may not be a good choice at the secondary level but may work well with preschool- or elementary-level students. Third, the signal is modeled so students know exactly what it is. Fourth, students practice the signal. Teachers can provide situations, such as taking attendance, in which the signal is given, students are expected to give the teacher attention, and the teacher thanks the students for getting quiet and listening, then takes attendance.

As with most classroom situations, signals should be changed and taught periodically. This maintains a novel climate in which motivation is more apparent.

Matching Intervention to Infraction: The Intervention Ladder

The conceptual framework for this book is best understood by studying the Intervention Ladder (see Figure 1.1), which graphically illustrates the hierarchy of disciplinary measures that educators can use to foster a positive learning environment. Because many educators have a penchant for selecting interventions that are complicated and do not fit the infractions, the Intervention Ladder can be a useful guide to aid in the selection of appropriate disciplinary actions. Prevention is the foundation of the ladder, based on the notion that educators should first try to prevent conduct problems. Prevention can be accomplished by rethinking the instructional content and activities, working together as a community to achieve consistent disciplinary responses to specific infractions, communicating carefully, and involving students as active participants in their total school program. If direct intervention becomes necessary, educators should select interventions on the lower rungs of the ladder before resorting to those found higher up. This requires a sensitive match between infractions and the intervention procedures that educators select. This process requires educators to continually evaluate the learning environment they have created, monitor their own actions, seek to prevent conduct problems, and intervene purposefully and systematically when the need arises. The selection of interventions aimed at reducing or eliminating violations of conduct codes should reflect a sensitivity to the seriousness of the infractions and the outcome of other mea-

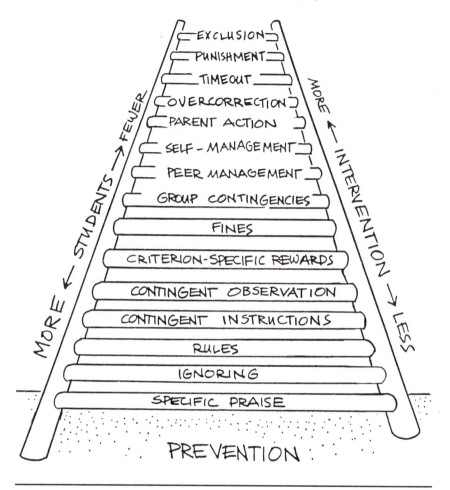

EXCLUSION
PUNISHMENT
TIMEOUT
OVERCORRECTION
PARENT ACTION
SELF-MANAGEMENT
PEER MANAGEMENT
GROUP CONTINGENCIES
FINES
CRITERION-SPECIFIC REWARDS
CONTINGENT OBSERVATION
CONTINGENT INSTRUCTIONS
RULES
IGNORING
SPECIFIC PRAISE

PREVENTION

FIGURE 1.1   The Intervention Ladder

sures tried earlier. Therefore, the interventions suggested in this book are arranged in a hierarchy in which mild interventions are selected first and more intrusive interventions are reserved for use only when other tactics have proven unsuccessful.

This approach requires educators to become activists. They cannot follow what Clarizio (1980) cleverly referred to over 10 years ago as the Pontius Pilate approach of washing their hands of disciplinary affairs. Educators must be actively involved in all aspects of creating and protecting a positive learning environment. They must seek to prevent conduct problems and intervene when situations mandate the application of direct disciplinary measures. To do this, educators must be fully aware of many different prevention and intervention techniques. They need to know about many diverse tactics that contribute to the creation and protection of a climate conducive to learning. Therefore, this book discusses the numerous procedures that educators can select to enhance student growth and learning.

Remembering Guiding Principles

Part of any good discipline program is awareness of and adherence to certain basic principles. These principles promote a good foundation upon which an effective discipline program is developed.

1. *Maintain "with-it-ness"*—This means that teachers know what is happening in their classrooms at all times. It requires that teachers have "eyes in the back of their heads" and let students know such is the case.

2. *Use the "ripple effect"*—This effect is seen when a teacher reinforces one student for raising his or her hand, and then other students raise their hands to speak. This effect can be positive or negative; teachers should focus on the positive (Kounin, 1970).

3. *Avoid power struggles*—There are no winners, and students may leave the situation feeling hostile and resentful.

4. *Give students choices*—Teachers must allow students to become involved in their educational programs by encouraging them to make decisions that pertain to their learning environment.

5. *Avoid grudges*—When the misbehavior and consequence are completed, the teacher should continue with positive interactions with the student.

6. *Focus on the students' behavior*—The teacher should ensure that all students understand that it is their behavior that is problematic and not them as individuals.

7. *Be prepared*—The teacher should have all teaching materials and lesson plans at hand so that time is not lost searching for misplaced materials or lesson activities.

8. *Avoid references to the past*—The teacher should start each day or period fresh with no reminders about previous disruptive behaviors.

9. *Anticipate problems*—This principle requires teachers to know their students and the curriculum so that students who

need extra assistance to succeed receive such instruction. Teachers also need to know how some students cope with transitional periods and social situations.

10. *Identify positive techniques for stress management*—Teachers must take time for themselves, leaving school situations and work behind temporarily.

DISCUSSION QUESTIONS

1. What are some ways teachers can exert their influence to maintain effective discipline?
2. Why is consistency such an important part of good discipline practices?
3. What are some techniques that promote good communication with parents and other teachers?
4. What is the philosophy of the intervention ladder? What are other interventions that could become part of the ladder?
5. How do teachers maintain "with-it-ness" while they are teaching small groups of students?

PRACTICE WHAT YOU'VE LEARNED

1. Discuss some of the societal issues that impact on education. Brainstorm ways to address these issues.
2. Identify some of the discipline concerns at your school. Describe ways in which these concerns are addressed.
3. Brainstorm indicators of a positive school climate. Discuss ways in which this climate is achieved.
4. Explain how all groups can be involved in school decision making when discipline practices are being determined.
5. List ways in which teachers can be consistent when disciplining students.
6. Establish your own list of guiding principles.

SUMMARY

1. Information about discipline as a national educational issue was presented. Concern about discipline remains a forefront

issue and must be addressed. Educators must identify constructive interventions to manage student conduct.

2. Developing a philosophy of discipline is an essential first step for establishing a positive disciplinary school climate.

3. Schoolwide discipline practices should be established. This includes promoting a positive school climate and involving all groups that are a part of the school community in making decisions about the learning environment.

4. Several instructional practices were discussed. The teacher sets the tone for the classroom and contributes to the school climate. Suggestions were provided to help teachers establish a good foundation for further effective discipline practices.

CHAPTER DISCUSSION ACTIVITIES

1. Identify factors pertaining to discipline as an issue in education.

2. What is your philosophy of discipline?

3. Describe ways to promote schoolwide effective discipline.

4. How can teachers lay the foundation for creating effective discipline practices in the classroom?

2

Preventing Disciplinary Problems

OBJECTIVES

After reading this chapter, you should be able to

1. Explain why behavior problems occur.

2. Describe types of disruptions that occur.

3. Discuss various circumstances that may promote behavior problems.

4. Identify instructional practices that contribute to disruptive behavior.

5. Discuss the importance of an appropriate student–curriculum match.

6. Describe the connection between motivation and behavior problems.

7. Identify effective practices for establishing rules.

8. Discuss problems that students with behavior disorders may exhibit.

9. Explain different interventions to prevent behavior problems.

10. Complete "Practice What You've Learned" activities.

Discipline ideas to be discussed in this chapter include

- **Why Behavior Problems Occur**
  Types of Disruptions
  Circumstances
  Instructional Procedures

21

SAINT PETER'S COLLEGE LIBRARY
JERSEY CITY, NEW JERSEY 07306

Boredom or Frustration
Motivation
Students with Behavioral Disorders
• **Preventive Interventions**
Teaching Students to Match Situations with Proper Behavioral Responses
Establishing Classroom Expectations
Managing the Environment
Planning for Transitions
Encouraging Academic Success
Creating an Exciting Learning Environment
Rescheduling Activities

Many conduct problems can be prevented and direct intervention avoided if educators more carefully analyze the learning environment. An understanding of why conduct problems occur can be helpful to determine whether the instructional content and activities should be altered or the code of conduct more thoroughly explained. Often, simple changes (e.g., different seating arrangements, more flexible academic schedules in the environment) reduce the level of disruption and distraction, thereby eliminating the need for direct intervention. Educators often implement complicated intervention programs unnecessarily. There is no reason to develop an elaborate point system for improved behavior when merely reviewing behavioral expectations and holding a class discussion about codes of conduct and what they specifically mean will remedy the situation.

Preventing conduct problems could be viewed as intervention. As such, it is located at the bottom of the Intervention Ladder to signify that teachers should implement preventive measures from day one. Preventive interventions should be considered before tactics listed on the Intervention Ladder are implemented. Only when the preventive measures discussed in this chapter prove unsuccessful should educators resort to the more intrusive procedures described in Chapters 3 and 4.

To develop an effective discipline plan, educators need to understand why behavior problems occur. Many behavior problems can be avoided if teachers recognize and respond to situations that might create problems in the classroom or school. Furthermore, teachers should be familiar with a variety of preventive measures that could minimize classroom disruptions.

WHY BEHAVIOR PROBLEMS OCCUR

Just as there are vast numbers of students who attend public schools today, there are equally vast numbers of reasons why individuals and groups do not conform to school rules and expectations. The most common ones are discussed briefly in the following sections.

Types of Disruptions

Almost all students exhibit some kind of discipline problem or disruptive behavior during their 13-year school career. It is the *kind, degree, place,* and *amount of disruption* that determines whether the behavior creates a problem for educators. Often, a fine line exists between what is acceptable deportment and what is not. Many students have difficulty understanding the limits of acceptable behavior (Krumboltz & Krumboltz, 1972). Frequently, school personnel do not help students learn how to make these subtle discriminations. For example, students must learn that it is appro-

priate to talk during group discussions, but it is not acceptable to interact verbally with peers during a film or lecture. They must learn that Ms. Larsen will tolerate a noisy class, but Mr. McDowell expects to be able to hear a pin drop. Students need to learn that it is expected for them to be active and talkative during gym class, but not during library time.

Educators must help students learn to discriminate among the behavioral options in each school situation and match that situation with the proper behavior pattern. Effectively matching the situation with the appropriate behavior pattern is an important skill to learn, because, when they are adults, students will need to know when they can acceptably engage in one kind of behavior pattern and when they cannot. For example, what is acceptable behavior at a football stadium is not at the grocery store. The deportment allowed in the neighborhood pub is most likely inappropriate in the boss' office. Therefore, some conduct problems occur simply because students do not know how to read the environmental cues—some subtle and some not so subtle—that indicate the acceptability of behavior.

Circumstances

Conduct problems sometimes occur because of the *circumstances*. For example, expecting a class of first graders to sit quietly for a symphony orchestra's hour-long rehearsal is probably unreasonable. It is just as unreasonable to expect bright students to sit and wait 20 minutes for the rest of the class to complete a seatwork assignment. Sometimes teachers misjudge the attention span of students and expect them to sit quietly for too long a time. Merely allowing students to move around and talk with their neighbors periodically, as a short break, will help avoid conduct difficulties.

Another circumstance that may be problematic is the arrangement of the environment. Sometimes behavior problems occur because traffic patterns are congested. This circumstance invites problems as students move about the classroom to different areas or in the hallway to other classrooms. Another environmental consideration is seating arrangements. Seating students together who do not get along or who tend to be talkative invites problems. Simply observing how students interact socially will help teachers make decisions about appropriate seating arrangements.

Transitional periods also may present problems. The circumstances dictate that students are (a) moving freely about the classroom from one activity to the next, (b) changing from one lesson to the next at their desks, or (c) lining up to go from the classroom to another area in the school. Emmer, Evertson, Sanford, Clements, and Worsham (1984) stated that transitional problems are due to a lack of (a) readiness, (b) expectations for acceptable behavior, or (c) effective procedures.

Instructional Procedures

Effective instructional procedures include practices that minimize behavior problems. Unfortunately, some instructional procedures are not emphasized sufficiently; thus, students are left to complete work independently when they are not ready to do so. For example, sometimes students are disruptive because they do not understand what is being taught and fail to ask for clarification. In other situations, the lesson may be too slow, allowing students time to create diversions to occupy their attention until the teacher is ready to move on to the next activity. Other times, concepts are not fully taught or modeled. A short introductory lesson followed by a paper-and-pencil assignment may leave some students unclear about the concept they must apply. Implementing effective instructional procedures (described below) can promote better student understanding and ability to complete assignments with minimal behavioral concerns.

Boredom or Frustration

Many problems occur because students are either bored with an activity that is too easy or frustrated because it is too difficult. One important study (Center, Deitz, & Kaufman, 1982) evaluated the relationship between task difficulty and inappropriate behavior. The relationship is dramatic and clear. When there is a mismatch between student ability and academic assignments, disruption occurs at a high level. Because of the results of their research, these investigators suggested that "when behavior problems arise in the classroom, one of the first factors to be examined should be instructional procedures and materials and their appropriateness to the

offending student" (p. 371). The need for flexible educational programming is a pervasive reality in today's schools. This is due to federal requirements to mainstream students with disabilities, to bus pupils to achieve social integration, and to not track or group students by ability. Because of these mandates, teachers must accommodate students with varying abilities and plan flexible activities that will hold the interest of diverse class members.

Motivation

Many students come to school with a well-developed ability to disrupt the learning atmosphere. These students know how to read the environmental cues and what the behavioral expectations are in various school settings. They are neither bored because the educational activity is too easy nor frustrated because it is too hard. For whatever reasons, they are not motivated to become active participants in the learning situation, but rather they seek to disrupt the learning climate. Their behavioral repertoires are counterproductive to their own and their classmates' learning. These students can be found in all types of educational programs: regular education, special education, title programs, and gifted or accelerated classes. Sometimes they display disruptive behavior patterns one year but not the next. Sometimes they disturb one or two classes but not others.

Because the behavior of only one student can destroy the learning environment for an entire class, assembly, gym period, or field trip, the behavior problem must be confronted. Although some of the preventive measures discussed in this chapter might be of sufficient power to encourage students to act appropriately, the likelihood is that many of these students will be candidates for more direct intervention procedures. Those procedures, presented in the next two chapters, might be necessary to ensure that the learning environment is not thrown out of balance by the disruptive few.

Students with Behavioral Disorders

Another group of students who attend public schools are the source of considerable disruption. These students typically are found within the special education population, but are included in regular classes in accordance with their abilities. These students seem unable to meet the behavioral expectations of typical classroom situations for extended periods of time. Their inability to conform, their frequent frustration over the learning activities, and the recognition by their peers that they are different often lead to disruptive situations. The students with the most severe behavioral disabilities often are mainstreamed only during recess, lunch, and other free periods. Although many of these students need a considerable amount of structure to meet setting demands, they are integrated into parts of the school day when the structure is at a minimum. Most likely, this contributes to their difficulties in meeting behavioral expectations. Because they are not part of the regular group—a fact that is verified by their absence during standard academic periods—they become easy targets for teasing and rebuff by the regular education students. When these students are the center of disruption, there are generally two different reasons for the disturbance. The first relates to the inability of these special education students to act appropriately. The second reason rests with their "normal" peers and the temptation to bait, chide, and encourage inappropriate behavior from these students. The procedures discussed throughout this text should reduce the disruption surrounding these students, but in most cases, direct intervention procedures, such as those discussed in later chapters, are required to keep them and their peer group under control.

An analysis of the causes of inappropriate school behaviors can help educators select specific preventive and intervention measures that reduce the likelihood of disruption. The preventive measures suggested in the remainder of this chapter should be integrated into the entire school management plan, not implemented only when discipline becomes a serious, schoolwide problem.

DISCUSSION QUESTIONS

1. What are examples of behaviors that are problematic in one location but not another?
2. Why are some behaviors viewed as disruptive by some teachers or administrators but not by others?
3. What are examples of matches and mismatches of behaviors and places?
4. What are examples of congested traffic patterns?
5. What environmental arrangements minimize behavior problems?
6. What role does "attention span" play in disruptive behaviors?
7. What are examples of effective instructional procedures?
8. How can an appropriate match between student and curriculum be accomplished?
9. What role does motivation play in disruptive behaviors?

PREVENTIVE INTERVENTIONS

Prevention is the foundation for any solid effective discipline plan. Preventive interventions require educators to examine closely the general structure of the school and classroom setting. This means that analysis of the educational environment must include basic classroom and school management techniques, curriculum, and instruction. First and foremost, educators must know their students. They must know student strengths and weaknesses behaviorally, socially, and academically. Only after educators learn about their students can they plan effective preventive interventions. This section focuses on interventions that tap classroom management, curriculum, and instruction. The common denominator across these areas is the needs of each student. Sound preventive measures based on a knowledge of individual students will establish a foundation for future interventions if they are necessary.

Teaching Students to Match Situations with Proper Behavioral Responses

Students must learn how to discriminate environmental situations and identify the appropriate behavioral responses for those situations. Some ways in which educators can help students learn this discrimination include the following:

1. Providing students with examples of behaviors and places. Students then tell if the behaviors are appropriate for the places. For example, "talking loudly" could be the behavior and the library could be the location. The teacher could help the students identify examples and nonexamples.

2. Having students make recommendations for good matches between behaviors and places.

3. Providing students with examples of degrees of behaviors, such as talking occasionally to talking constantly. Students identify when and where different degrees of behaviors are acceptable.

4. Having students identify how rules change according to the place and person. For instance, one set of rules may exist in fourth-period class and another set during third-period class. Likewise, one set of rules may exist for hallway behavior and another for cafeteria time.

Educators can use modeling, role playing, and reinforcement to teach these environmental discriminations and behavioral response matches. Additionally, educators should talk to one another to determine if such instruction is generalizing across classrooms and teachers.

Establishing Classroom Expectations

Although *rules* is listed on the Intervention Ladder, it is important to note that establishing codes of conduct is also a necessary component of any good prevention program. Such expectations provide students with guidelines for what is and is not acceptable behavior in the classroom and school. Teachers who do not have a set of expectations for classroom behavior invite behavior problems because students do not know what is required of them. Codes of conduct should be concise and clearly articulated. They should be stated in a positive manner and developed with student participation. These expectations should be conveyed to parents and members of the school community. It is also important that they be enforced consistently with appropriate positive or negative consequences. Specific information about developing classroom rules is presented in Chapter 3.

Managing the Environment

Several factors should be examined when managing the environment to prevent discipline problems. First, traffic areas are prime opportunities for students to talk to each other, engage in physical contact, and become involved in disruptive behaviors. These areas include certain locations in the classroom that students frequent, such as the pencil sharpener, restrooms, water fountain, and pathways. Teachers can prevent possible problems by (a) keeping areas separated, (b) providing plenty of space, and (c) ensuring that areas have easy access (Evertson, Emmer, Clements, Sanford, & Worsham, 1984). Teachers can plan activities for students to complete independently, which necessitate some movement about the room, and watch how well traffic patterns work. Through this analysis, teachers can pinpoint potential problem areas and rearrange furniture or work area locations to prevent problems.

Second, class seating arrangements require careful consideration to minimize behavior problems. Teachers must know students well enough to determine who gets along with one another, who the "talkers" are, and who needs to be alone to complete assignments. A second part of making a seating arrangement decision focuses on the desk arrangement. For example, some teachers prefer groups of desks, whereas others like desks in rows. Each arrangement style represents a philosophy of how students learn and interact best. For example, desks in rows is a traditional seating arrangement, implying that the teacher stands in front of the classroom and lectures. Although opportunity exists for discussion, students do not have the opportunity to engage in small-group work or to learn social skills. On the other hand, grouping desks means that students can work together and socialize when appropriate; however, these students must be able to complete their independent work while sitting together. Some teachers have carrels in which students sit at their desks with a barrier surrounding three sides. This barrier limits the distractions that cause certain students to become disruptive or impede their ability to complete their work. Whatever arrangement is chosen probably will change as the school year progresses. Students learn to work better under certain circumstances, and seating arrangements must be adjusted to meet the changing environmental demands.

Third, materials to be used by students or teachers during instruction should be readily accessible to minimize lost instructional time spent locating missing materials and to keep students more actively involved. Time spent by the teacher securing materials for lessons at the beginning or end of the day can reduce the probability of disruptive behaviors occurring during instruction while the teacher is busy locating materials. Also, students should be taught how to use any audiovisual equipment that is part of a center or work area. The time spent instructing students on how to use and handle equipment properly will reduce unengaged time, interruptions, and behavior problems.

Planning for Transitions

Teachers can conduct an exciting lesson in which students are actively involved and on task, yet seconds later, after the lesson concludes, chaos can erupt. The primary reason for this scenario is the teacher's lack of planning for the transition to the next activity. Perhaps students were not ready for the transition; the teacher provided no warning about getting ready or no instructions for the students to know how to proceed appropriately. These situations invite behavior problems, yet are easily remedied.

Effective transition planning requires several steps. First, teachers should provide a readiness signal telling students that it is time to finish their work. They should be told, for instance, that in 10 minutes it will be time to line up for the library, to go to lunch, or for the bell to ring. This prepares students for a pending transition to another in-class activity or school location.

Second, teachers should gain student attention before any transition occurs. A signal, as described in Chapter 1, can be used. Teachers can then review what students just completed and preview what will happen next. This time frame gives students a chance to quiet down; however, this period should be brief to maintain attention.

Third, teachers should tell students how they are to make a transition (e.g., line up starting with the first row, with students wearing blue, or with students whose last names begin with A through F) and what the behavioral expectations are (e.g., walk quietly, do not talk, keep hands to yourself, stay in a straight line, have all materials on top of desk).

Fourth, teachers should provide positive reinforcement for students who follow the transition plan. A negative consequence should be imposed for students who are unable to follow the plan.

Encouraging Academic Success

Teachers can promote student academic success by focusing on effective instructional procedures and accurate academic productivity. Instructional procedures are techniques used to present content to students. It is important for teachers to employ techniques that will enable students to comprehend and master instructional content, thus minimizing boredom, frustration, and behavior problems.

✔ **RESEARCH TO PRACTICE—1.**   Researchers (e.g., Bickel & Bickel, 1986; Rieth, Polsgrove, & Semmel, 1981; Rivera & Smith, 1987; Smith, 1989) have shown consistently that certain techniques enhance student learning abilities. These techniques include

1. Modeling and imitating

2. Defining concepts

3. Checking for student understanding

4. Pacing

5. Guiding students in practice situations

6. Monitoring and adjusting instruction

7. Providing independent practice opportunities

8. Using advance organizers

9. Evaluating instruction

10. Engaging students in instruction; minimizing "down time"

Not only must teachers provide direct instruction to teach concepts, but they must work with students who are practicing newly acquired information and check periodically that students understand what they are doing. Only then are students ready to move into an independent practice mode. In other words, telling students how to do the math problems, modeling one or two examples on the chalkboard, and having students complete 50 problems independently is not an example of effective instruction. Students must be taught, monitored, and evaluated to ensure content mastery and reduce behavioral disruptions.

Educators must strive to help students obtain academic productivity. Yet for some students, off-task behavior reduces their ability to achieve this goal. Thus, some teachers try to increase students' on-task behavior to promote more work completion. Although this may be appealing intuitively, researchers have shown that helping students obtain academic productivity requires a direct approach. The findings of several academic research studies clearly demonstrate the relationship between academic and social behaviors. Knowledge of this relationship is critical and avoids the necessity of employing discipline measures at school for many students. It is truly a prevention concept.

✔ **RESEARCH TO PRACTICE—2.** During the early 1970s, two groups of researchers (Ayllon & Roberts, 1974; Ferritor, Buckholdt, Hamblin, & Smith, 1972) made interesting and important discoveries. In two well-controlled studies, these researchers compared the relationship between increased academic performance and reduced amount of time spent off task. In each experiment, during one condition the students were reinforced for increasing their academic output (concurrently the amount of time spent off task was measured). The results from both experiments were similar. In Ayllon and Roberts's research, for example, the students were initially disruptive 34% of the time and their level of accuracy was below 50%. When reinforcement was initiated for improved academic performance, disruption dropped to less than 15% and accuracy improved to 70%. When academic output was targeted to increase, it did, and off-task behavior decreased. However, in the Ferritor et al. study, when attending was reinforced, it increased, but arithmetic accuracy did not. It seems that students can appear to be paying attention, but not really be focusing their attention on the task at hand.

Although these two studies have received attention, many educators and researchers still believe that attention to task is an important variable that contributes to academic success. However, after a series of studies in which Hallahan and his associates analyzed the relationship between attention to task and academic productivity, they reversed their original premise:

> Apparently, regardless of the intervention procedure used, a consistent bidirectional positive relationship does not exist between attention to task and academic productivity.... [T]he treatment of academic pro-

ductivity will have beneficial side effects on attention to task . . . while treatment of attention to task may have such effects. (Lloyd, Hallahan, Kosiewicz, & Kneedler, 1982, p. 226)

The results of these three studies provide educators with two important pieces of information. On the one hand, increased attention by teachers, administrators, and parents to academic performance should result in less disruption during academic periods. In other words, if incentives (e.g., praise, contests, earned privileges, free time) are provided for increased academic productivity or more accurate academic performance, less off-task or disruptive behavior will result. On the other hand, focusing efforts to reduce off-task performance (e.g., being out of one's seat, talking out of turn, daydreaming) will cause an increase in on-task behavior, but may not produce an increase in academic performance. Certainly, academic improvement is of the utmost concern to educators. Because the reason for keeping disruption to a minimum is to enhance the educational process, the correlation demonstrated by these findings between academic improvement and the reduction of disruption is encouraging.

Many educators have observed this phenomenon. Recently, a concern has emerged about the academic achievement of students in the public school system. Therefore, many administrators, particularly principals, have encouraged teachers and students to raise the schoolwide average scores on annual achievement tests. Some principals have even entered into contests with other principals to see which school could raise achievement levels the most. Those who work in schools in which academic achievement is stressed commonly observe that the level of disruption decreases without much direct effort by teachers and other school personnel.

Creating an Exciting Learning Environment

One merely needs to think about those who rarely create discipline problems to realize a common characteristic of many of these students: They are actively involved in various aspects of school life. They are academic achievers who are excited about the learning opportunities presented to them. They are members of the schools' governing body. They are participants in extracurricular activities (e.g., orchestra, drama, athletics, clubs). These students find things that interest them. They become active participants in the overall educational process. Although these students are not always interested in every required academic subject or school function in which participation is expected, their overall conduct typically is acceptable because they are active members of the school community. This type of participation provides them with the motivation to come to school as willing and cooperative members.

Unfortunately, school does not have this appeal for all students. Only those who demonstrate academic interest and ability are included actively in the content of school curricula. Only those who seek participation in special school groups and exhibit skills in those areas are included as members of special groups. In the large schools, which have become commonplace in American public education, only the very few can become so involved. For example, in secondary schools, only the top 5% can become part of the honor society, and only a limited number can be on the basketball team or serve as cheerleaders. So it goes; despite the size of the school, only a limited number can become involved in traditional, organized, school-sponsored activities. Similar examples can be cited in elementary and middle schools. The larger the school, the larger the number of those who cannot qualify for participation and, therefore, the larger number of inactive participants. Many inactive participants become disillusioned with school and see no reason to conform to school rules or policies. Some of these youth seek groups of their own in which they can be recognized and involved. These unofficial groups often become gangs, in which conforming to school expectations is not respected or desired.

For many, school is not exciting, fun, or meaningful. Unfortunately, as disciplinary problems increase, there is a concurrent decrease in the enjoyable and interesting aspects of school life. As externally imposed authority is viewed necessary by educators, the motivation for becoming an active learner lessens. Classroom instruction becomes more rigid, allowing less room for creative thinking. The fun of being in school lessens. The result of this cycle is frustrating: Discipline, instead of improving, worsens.

Based on the premise that students involved in the learning process and in school-based activities are less likely to engage in disruption, educators need to use their creativity to develop more ways for all to become actively involved in classroom and school affairs. However, teachers are finding it increasingly difficult to interest students today. They must compete with a world that provides multisensory stimulation and excitement. American homes are filled with television and stereo systems. Those who exercise or jog no longer merely exercise, but do it to music. All aspects of American life are changing to make things more exciting and enjoyable. Arcades and home microcomputers entice students with challenging video games. By comparison, many schools are lacking. They are replete with dry lectures, old and outdated educational films, books with difficult content, and an overly structured format.

CLASSROOM LEARNING ACTIVITIES. To make learning fun and exciting is much more of a challenge today than it was only a few years ago. Although it is distasteful for some teachers to realize that they are competing with the world outside of school, they must find ways to entice students into the learning process just as video games have enticed them. This is a modern reality that must be faced, a challenge that can be met. Within each classroom setting, the teacher must become aware of this competition and rethink the format for presenting information. Teachers must evaluate their own styles and think of new ways to change their presentations, and thereby involve students in the learning situation. Students can also offer good suggestions about ways that would involve them more in the learning process.

Many methods can be devised to encourage students' involvement in the educational process. It is up to teachers and their classes to create exciting learning experiences, so only a few examples that might stimulate thought about how the curriculum could be adapted are presented in the remainder of this chapter.

> Mr. Pohland had been teaching American history, a required course for graduation, for 15 years. He used the state-adopted American history textbook, supplemented by films on the American Revolution and World War II. He had used the same lectures and examinations for years. After so many years of teaching the same subject to students who were required to attend, he and his class were bored and felt that each semester was something to be endured. Each year he had more deportment problems, and he firmly believed that this was due to the lack of interest by today's youth in his subject matter. For his mental well-being, he decided to change the way he presented some of the material. After all, through lectures, he was merely spoon-feeding his captive audience. He decided that one of his American history classes should dig out the facts for themselves to truly understand Revolutionary times and the persons who had set the course for future American action.
>
> He decided that one way to achieve his aim was to have the class write, produce, and perform a play that characterized the real people who were shapers of American history. He brought in his personal library, which included biographies and critical analyses of the times. He took his class to the school library to find more books related to the issues and subjects. He required them to go to the public library to find out more about the central characters of the play the class was to produce. All of the students were involved. The most able readers were to handle and condense the difficult material for the rest of the class. The more artistic students were to develop, with the aid of various small groups, historically accurate sets and costumes. The class became consumed with the project: All members had a key role in creating, producing, and executing the play. They all became active participants in the project, they learned substantially about that period of American history, and disruption was greatly reduced.

Of course, all teachers in a school cannot use the same method for encouraging student involvement in a subject. If every teacher decided to use a student play to facilitate curricular involvement, the novelty would diminish, as would student interest. Numerous other activities can be selected:

1. Have students become roving journalists who report historical events or interview authors of major writings.

2. Invite community resource persons as guest lecturers on specific aspects of science or mathematics.

3. Plan for groups studying computer programming to visit a local business that manages information by using a microcomputer.

4. Arrange for classes studying a particular playwright to attend a rehearsal or performance of that author's work.

The number of special activities that could encourage greater participation is almost limitless. Teachers, however, need flexibility and creativity. The implementation of anything different from the standard instructional format that prevails in many American classrooms today requires thought and planning. Duplication of special activities will eventually make these activities as unchallenging as the traditional instructional format. To avoid duplication, teachers within a school should meet and coordinate these activities. For example, each department could meet to share ideas for diverse and stimulating activities. Then, representatives of each department could meet and share those special activities planned for each academic area to ensure that no one enrichment activity is overused during any school year with the same group of students.

SCHOOLWIDE LEARNING ACTIVITIES. Just as educators can adjust instructional activities to include more students as active participants, they can devise methods for increasing schoolwide student involvement. As mentioned earlier, today's schools allow proportionately few opportunities for student involvement; however, this situation is valid only if the traditional view of extracurricular activities is taken. Although only a set number of students can participate on each athletic team or in the school orchestra, there are many other areas of school life that allow the active involvement of the student population. Many activities are time-consuming to the school personnel assigned these responsibilities and, unfortunately, others are left undone because of the shortage of extra personnel in these times of financial constraints.

> Ms. Wood, principal of Hawthorne School, found that the litter around campus was appalling. She discussed this problem with the other principals in the district and found that this was not an uncommon problem. Due to the lack of funds, the school district could not afford to provide extra maintenance crews to clean playgrounds and schoolyards. In fact, Ms. Wood was lucky to have the extra custodian required to clean her school's buildings. Ms. Wood decided that the problem must be attacked, but it would have to be without paid personnel. She requested volunteers for a blue-ribbon task force of students to suggest ideas to help reduce the amount of litter around school. The first 10 students who volunteered were put on the task force.
>
> The group brainstormed ideas and met with students in other classes to gather ideas on the matter. After several weeks of working with students in the school, the task force developed an implementation plan. The group met with Ms. Wood and discussed the feasibility of each idea suggested and jointly set a plan of action. An implementation team was then organized. Three schoolwide contests were planned: one for an antilitter slogan, another for a drawing or logo for the trash receptacles, and a third for advertising posters to be placed around the school. Ms. Wood then asked for volunteers for two more teams: a study team to determine where the trash receptacles should be placed and a data collection team. The study team was limited to 12 students, but all those who volunteered for the data collection team were accepted. The data team elected a captain. Each Friday afternoon, the members picked up and counted the litter from the grounds. They reported this tally to the team captain, who kept a weekly record of the number of items that littered the school building and grounds. Another group volunteered to

repaint the trash receptacles. After 3 weeks, the antilittering slogan, logo, posters, and trash receptacles were in place. On the basis of the litter collected by Ms. Wood's data collection team and the general appearance of the school, it became clear that the plan was working. Very little litter was left on the grounds for the data team to collect and count each Friday. Ms. Wood's goal was accomplished: Her campus was no longer unsightly, and the students tended to litter the grounds substantially less.

The primary reason, however, for the success of Ms. Wood's project was the active involvement of the school community. Antilittering became not only Ms. Wood's concern, but the school community's concern as well. In fact, her goal was better met with this method than by employing extra maintenance personnel, which could have subtracted from the instructional budget.

Charles (1981) added a very pertinent point about students' growth and its relationship to discipline: the need for students to develop a sense of responsibility.

> Students acquire this sense of responsibility through being put into responsible situations. When they must be accountable for their actions, for keeping the classroom neat and orderly, for meeting assignments, for helping others, and so forth, they learn that they are responsible for their own acts. This sense of responsibility grows slowly, but its long-range effects are important. (p. 11)

This sense of responsibility prevents students from engaging in many kinds of disruption. Such responsibility can be fostered only when students are encouraged to be active participants in the learning environment.

In most schools today, the chances for such participation are minimal. Some ways to increase involvement through various learning activities include

1. Involving more winners in school contests

2. Expanding student governance to include more students

3. Creating special task forces to deal with problems faced by the entire school community

4. Having students assume responsibilities for tasks that teachers must now add to already full schedules

5. Conducting an informal analysis to determine how more active involvement can be achieved

Each school's administrative staff (e.g., principal, vice principal), together with a group of interested teachers, could devise ways to ease teachers' workloads and involve more students in school.

Rescheduling Activities

Many teachers notice that discipline problems occur more frequently at specific times within academic periods. There is nothing earthshaking about this observation. Students simply have preferences about instructional activities. During those activities that interest them, students are less disruptive. During those that are less interesting, students act out more. As discussed earlier, it is best to keep uninteresting, monotonous tasks to a minimum. Regardless of the efforts made by teachers, however, some aspects of the instructional program are not intrinsically fun or motivating to all students. No matter how much effort is put into creating exciting instructional tasks, some learning requires drill and practice. All monotony cannot be avoided. Students often express their interest, and indirectly their disinterest, in specific instructional tasks. They reveal their preferences by asking such questions as "Could we do choral reading first today?" implying that they like to do seatwork assignments less.

One well-researched and efficacious principle that applies to this situation is referred to as the Premack Principle (Premack, 1959). This is a scheduling method by which the least preferred activities are completed successfully before students are allowed to engage in preferred activities. For example, once their arithmetic worksheets are completed correctly, students may spend time as they wish (e.g., reading their library books, working on independent projects).

Because many students while away time during the scheduling of non-preferred activities, thereby wasting valuable instructional time, some educators have modified the Premack Principle: If the time that students waste during low-preference activities can be recaptured for instructional purposes, the students can spend some of it in an activity of their choice. Teachers who adhere to this notion allow students the opportunity to earn free time. Free time (or earned time), an extension of the Premack Principle, is based on the assumption that allowing students to spend time as they would like (with certain constraints, of course) after they have successfully completed the instructional assignments serves as a reward for more accurate and quickly completed assignments.

> Mr. Sanchez found that his class was most disruptive during spelling. The students were to do the daily workbook assignments provided in basal spellers during the 30-minute daily spelling period. Many of his pupils daydreamed. The brighter ones, who completed the seatwork

assignments faster than their classmates, disturbed the rest of the class for the remainder of the period. Generally, Mr. Sanchez felt that too much time was devoted to spelling and that it was a source of general disruption. Mr. Sanchez implemented a free-time plan. He told the class that 25 minutes each day would be devoted to spelling exercises, but once any student completed the assignment correctly and quietly, he or she would have the remainder of the period free. During free time, students could do activities of their choice. Two students could work together on a project, but they had to be quiet so as not to disturb the others. Mr. Sanchez found that he had regained 5 minutes of instructional time and overall spelling performance improved.

✔ **RESEARCH TO PRACTICE.**   Free time, when contingently applied, has helped improve academic and nonacademic school-related tasks. In one study (Cowen, Jones, & Bellack, 1979), which included students from five regular elementary classrooms, disruption was reduced substantially when students could earn free time for not being disruptive and not wasting instructional time. There are definite reasons why free time works so successfully across chronological ages and grade levels:

1. It serves as a reward for completing assignments accurately and not disturbing the class during work time.

2. It does not allow students to have idle time. When work is completed, each student may select other constructive activities in which to engage.

3. The chosen activity can be changed. One day a student may want to read a book, but another day may choose to solve a crossword puzzle.

Because of the variety of activities for selection, students do not seem to tire of free time. Because they may select activities that interest them, the tactic is not age specific. Rather, it appeals to students across the school years.

DISCUSSION QUESTIONS

1. What are factors to consider when getting to know your students?
2. How are seating arrangements established?

3. How can educators arrange classrooms to establish effective traffic patterns?
4. What are some do's and don'ts about transition plans?
5. What are examples of types of disruptions that are problematic in some instances and not in others?
6. What are ways that students can practice activities under the guidance of the teacher?
7. What are examples of independent practice activities?
8. What are ways educators can create learning environments that will appeal to and motivate students?
9. How can administrators help to create exciting learning environments?
10. What are examples of rules that promote effective discipline?

PRACTICE WHAT YOU'VE LEARNED

1. Brainstorm examples of types of disruptive behaviors. Propose techniques to teach students ways to match situations with behavioral responses.
2. Role play how students can be taught to examine situations and make appropriate behavioral responses.
3. Discuss behaviors that may indicate that student attention is waning during a lesson.
4. Draw a diagram of your classroom. Indicate high traffic patterns. Identify areas that are problematic, and propose solutions to lessen congested areas.
5. Devise a lesson to teach students a mathematics skill using the instructional procedures described in the preventive section under "Encouraging Academic Success."
6. Explain different ways to monitor student progress and to check for understanding.
7. Brainstorm behaviors that may indicate student boredom or frustration. Discuss ways to prevent and alleviate the boredom and frustration.
8. Make a list of your students. Briefly list their strengths and weaknesses. Describe preventive interventions for each student.
9. Brainstorm exciting and novel ways to teach social studies and science lessons.

10. Explain how you would apply the Premack Principle in your classroom.
11. Identify any transition problems that you face currently. Describe a transition plan to address those problems.
12. Explain how you prepare students for transition and what procedures you use to ensure success.
13. Describe schoolwide behavior problems that can be addressed using some of the preventive interventions discussed in this chapter.

SUMMARY

Discipline, a major problem facing educators, must be achieved if today's schools are to accomplish the important task of preparing students to meet the challenges of the next century. Due in part to the information explosion occurring in all areas of the curriculum, as well as the sophistication of society, demands upon educators have increased substantially. Instructional time is precious and must not be wasted because of conduct problems. The learning environment must foster the academic and social development of all American youth. This environment is delicate and can easily be destroyed by the discipline problems of a few. Undoubtedly, direct intervention procedures must be implemented to ensure the protection of this environment, but their necessity can be reduced through good schoolwide prevention methods.

The following points both summarize the content presented thus far in this book and serve as reminders of a commonsense approach to the prevention of conduct difficulties in school settings:

1. A positive learning environment can be fostered in all school settings.

2. The learning environment must be carefully guarded and protected so that students are free to discover, explore, investigate, create, solve problems, and learn maximally.

3. The delicate learning environment must not stifle but rather must foster the social and educational growth of students.

4. Educators must communicate carefully and clearly to students about expected behavior in school, and learn to exert their influence.

5. By adjusting and modifying instructional methods, teachers can eliminate many of the reasons for disruption and avoid the necessity for intervention.

6. Students who are active learners and involved in the school community are less likely to disrupt the learning environment.

7. Prevention measures should be integrated into a comprehensive school plan and not be implemented only when discipline is a problem.

8. Rescheduling educational activities so that the least preferred activities precede the more desired ones can prevent conduct problems.

9. Improved academic achievement should be encouraged, and all efforts and progress made by individual students should be recognized.

10. When all members of the school community (e.g., students, parents, educators, and staff) are actively involved—either through setting behavioral standards, selecting and implementing disciplinary measures, or being part of a community-wide communication network—a positive educational environment is more likely to be supported.

11. Better discipline is achieved when all who oversee school conduct do so systematically and consistently.

CHAPTER DISCUSSION ACTIVITIES

1. Why do behavior problems occur?

2. List types of disruptions that occur.

3. What circumstances may promote behavior problems?

4. What instructional practices contribute to disruptive behavior?

5. Why is an appropriate student–curriculum match important?

6. Describe the connection between motivation and behavior problems.

7. Discuss effective practices for establishing rules.

8. What types of problems may students with behavior disorders exhibit?

9. Explain different interventions to prevent behavior problems.

BEHAVIORS AND INTERVENTIONS

1. Identify specific target behaviors from your own experience. Describe preventive interventions from this chapter that will address the target behaviors. Share your information with others to gain additional ideas.

2. Describe a preventive intervention from this chapter that addresses the following behaviors:

- Likes to talk to other students

- Talks loudly

- Sharpens pencil frequently

- Pokes students on the way to the restroom

- Finishes math slowly

- Has difficulty standing in line

- Has a short attention span

- Talks to students in work areas

- Is easily frustrated

- Tends to finish work quickly

- Is easily interrupted when working

3

The Intervention Ladder, Part 1

OBJECTIVES

After reading this chapter, you should be able to

1. Explain reasons for using interventions on the lower part of the ladder.

2. Define mild and positive forms of direct intervention.

3. Explain how and when to implement the interventions.

4. Cite research to support the efficacy of the interventions.

5. Provide examples of when to use the interventions.

6. Participate in "Practice What You've Learned" opportunities.

Interventions to be discussed in this chapter include

- **Specific Praise**
- **Ignoring**
- **Rules**
- **Contingent Instructions**
- **Contingent Observation**
- **Criterion-Specific Rewards**
- **Fines**
- **Group Contingencies**

All members of the school community undoubtedly would like to live and work in an educational environment in which all have an unrelenting desire for knowledge, are challenged and excited about the educational materials provided, and are active participants in a positive school atmosphere. If such an atmosphere is not present naturally, it must be shaped and encouraged. School discipline is part of that atmosphere, for without it the learning climate is damaged for all students.

There are many ways of achieving discipline; some result in a positive climate and some do not. Many positive suggestions for preventing disruption have been offered already in this book, but preventive measures are not always sufficient. Often when these tactics are not successful, school personnel resort to unpleasant or punitive methods. The results of using these procedures often extend beyond the immediate punishment of those who caused the infraction and can have a serious long-term impact on the climate of the school, particularly if these methods become commonplace. Punitive tactics are easy to overuse, for they are expedient and sometimes seem to require the least effort by school personnel. Unfortunately, they do not always work with any permanence and, therefore, tend to be used repeatedly. The result of this cycle is not desirable for anyone. The one who administers the punitive procedures is, in the eyes of the students, a punitive person; however, more importantly, the school environment becomes repressive and negative, which is incompatible with most educators' ideals. What is the alternative? Clearly, disruption and violations of school codes must be dealt with directly, but punitive tactics should be held in reserve for those serious infractions that are not eliminated through other, more positive methods.

Educators can use many mild and positive forms of direct intervention when the learning environment is disturbed and preventive measures have proven unsuccessful. It is always important to remember that the learning environment is more positive and conducive to student growth if the implementation of severe and intrusive disciplinary measures is kept to a minimum.

The Intervention Ladder (see Chapter 1) was designed to illustrate an important concept. When direct intervention is necessary, tactics lower on the ladder match and serve to remediate a large number of behavioral incidents. They should be used first. Unfortunately, methods too stringent for specific behavioral infractions are often implemented before other tactics are tried. There are many reasons for this. Some school personnel tend to overreact to students' disruptive behavior or infractions of the school's code of conduct. Sometimes, preventive measures were not applied early enough to avoid the development of an unacceptable behavioral pattern. Finally, some educators are not thoroughly aware of the wide variety of interventions that are available, many of which are mild and do not seriously impair the learning environment.

Educators must match the intervention with the infraction. The Intervention Ladder should be helpful in this regard, for it illustrates a hierarchy of intervention categories and their severity. Tactics found lower on the ladder should be tried first. If evaluation of their effectiveness (see Chapter 5) indicates that mild methods are not successful, then tactics found higher on the ladder should be implemented. The Intervention Ladder illustrates the organization of this and the next chapter, and provides the conceptual framework for discussions about direct intervention procedures.

TIPS FOR IMPLEMENTATION

1. Identify and apply preventive measures as much as possible.

2. Match intervention to infraction.

3. Select mild and positive forms of direct intervention lower on the ladder first.

4. Evaluate the effectiveness of the intervention regularly.

PRACTICE WHAT YOU'VE LEARNED

1. Review the interventions discussed in this chapter by studying the Glossary for the Intervention Ladder, Part I (Table 3.3 in the chapter summary). For example, conceal the list of interventions. Read the examples and identify the intervention being described. Provide other examples for each intervention. Also, read the definitions and identify the intervention.

2. Discuss reasons for using mild and positive forms of direct intervention first.

3. Discuss reasons for the overuse of stringent, more punitive interventions without trying mild and positive forms of direct intervention.

4. Identify ways a school staff can focus on using mild and positive forms of interventions.

5. Identify specific behaviors, in the classroom and schoolwide, that can be handled with mild and positive interventions.

SPECIFIC PRAISE

DEFINITION

Specific praise means to provide students with positive statements and feedback about their appropriate conduct.

Praise, the intervention on the bottom rung of the Intervention Ladder, is interesting because it is simple to apply yet complex in nature. Because it is easy to use and has seemingly natural qualities, particularly in classroom and school settings, many consider it more preventive than an intervention. However, when used correctly, it has a powerful effect on behavior. In this sense, *direct* and *specific* are the key concepts to remember. When praise is given a student, it should be specific to the desired performance. Such praise can be provided in writing or verbally and publicly or privately. Keeping in mind the student for whom the praise is intended dictates the nature of delivery. Also, teachers should remember that when this intervention is initially utilized, it must be applied each time the targeted behavior occurs. As the students learn the desired expectation, specific praise can be applied intermittently. The vignettes that follow the Discussion Questions illustrate the effective use of specific praise.

DISCUSSION QUESTIONS

1. What are examples of behaviors for which specific praise is appropriate?

2. What are some ways to give specific praise at the preschool, elementary, and secondary levels?

3. What are some ways to provide specific praise verbally and in writing?

4. What are some examples of specific praise in reading, writing, mathematics, and social behavior?

The comment "Michael, you certainly had a good day today" is neither specific nor direct. However, a comment such as "Michael, thank you for returning from recess and beginning your work independently" is specific to the expected performance and direct in regard to the student's behavior that day.

The secondary-level teacher approaches a student and quietly comments, "Sarah, I appreciate your effort in coming to class on time and bringing all of your materials. It must feel good to know you're prepared for class." This statement tells the student specifically what she has done that meets the expectations of the teacher and the setting.

Mark was able to work quietly for an hour without disturbing his neighbors. The teacher wrote a quick note saying, "I appreciate how quietly you have been working this morning without talking to your neighbors" and placed it on his desk. She caught his eye after he read the note, smiled, and began working with another student.

Ms. Jones, the kindergarten teacher, thanked Alexandra, Ryan, and Samantha for coming to the carpet area for story time the first time she called. Others quickly joined the students in the carpet area.

Praise, although often consisting only of a phrase or short sentence, includes several important features. First, the student is given attention and positive comment about the desired or expected behavior. Second, specific praise takes the form of feedback regarding expected school decorum. This feature is important for many students, for they often do not truly understand what is expected from them. They have not fully integrated the unspoken rules of conduct. For them, the feedback aspect of specific praise serves in both an instructional and reinforcing role.

TIPS FOR IMPLEMENTATION

1. Identify the target student and behavior.

2. Gain attention.

3. Provide a positive comment about the desired or expected behavior.

4. Make the comment specific to the behavior.

5. Do this publicly or privately depending upon the situation and the student.

6. Provide specific praise orally or in writing.

7. Evaluate the effectiveness of the intervention regularly.

✔ **RESEARCH TO PRACTICE.** Although praise is a powerful and extremely easy tactic to employ, it is underutilized. The results of one research study are particularly shocking and disappointing. White (1975) studied the classroom manner of 104 teachers to determine their rates of approving and disapproving comments to students. She found a remarkable correlation between the number of positive (praise) statements and the grade level. Teachers of early elementary students had the highest approval and disapproval rates; they both criticized and praised their students regularly. After second grade, the rates declined sharply, and by middle school, students were reprimanded more often than they were praised. A class of eighth-grade students received as few as four positive comments per academic period. In high school, students heard even fewer positive or negative comments about their classroom behavior from teachers. These teachers seemed to have little to say to their students aside from content lectures. The results of White's study indicate that, once students enter middle school, they do not receive much praise, specific or otherwise. One of the simplest tactics available for better discipline remains untapped. Certainly, the climate of many classrooms and schools would be more positive if teachers and school personnel made the small efforts required to praise, thereby reminding their students what is expected.

PRACTICE WHAT YOU'VE LEARNED

1. Create examples of specific praise. Contrast these examples with praise that is not specific. An instance of specific praise might be "Thank you for working quietly on your assignments while I am working with this math group," whereas an example of nonspecific praise might be "Thank you for helping me out while I'm working with this math group." In this case, students are not told *specifically* what they are doing that is "helping out" the teacher.

2. Develop a plan of how to increase the use of specific praise in your classroom. Consider when and how specific praise would be used during instruction and transition. Identify a method for evaluating the effectiveness of your program (see Chapter 5).

3. Target a student for whom this intervention might be effective in changing an inappropriate behavior. Identify the inappropriate behavior, conduct baseline, identify when specific praise will be used, implement the intervention specific praise, and evaluate the effectiveness of the program.

4. Explain how the "ripple effect" and the use of specific praise could change student behaviors.

5. Identify when and how specific praise can be used as a schoolwide intervention.

IGNORING

DEFINITION

Ignoring means to systematically and consistently not pay attention to each occurrence of the target behavior.

Like specific praise, ignoring is a mild intervention. Although it can be powerful, it is applicable only in certain situations. Ignoring—the systematic withdrawal of attention when an undesirable behavior occurs—is effective only when the person whose attention is important to the target individual is the one who withholds attention. This awareness is very important, and should serve as a guide for the situations in which it is applied. The following two examples should illustrate this concept.

> Lee bothered all of the students around him during study hall. He told jokes to whomever would listen, pulled Carol's hair when she sat in front of him, sang songs, and constantly banged books and made noise. Mr. Hammill, the study hall teacher, decided to ignore Lee's noise and disruption. Unfortunately, Lee's behavior only worsened.
>
> Debra, a nursery school student, played with her classmates on the playground or participated in various group play activities only occasionally. Her teacher, Ms. Chavez, went to her often when she played alone and tried to encourage her to play with the other students; Debra continued to play alone most of the time. Then Ms. Chavez decided to change her plan. Each time Debra played with another student, Ms. Chavez went to Debra and the other student and talked with them about their play activities. Soon Debra rarely played alone, and she became more involved with the other students in her class.

In the first example, the teacher's ignoring Lee's disruption did not achieve the desired result for two reasons. First, the teacher's attention was not what Lee wanted. Lee desired and received the attention of the students around him in study hall. For ignoring to have worked in Lee's situation, the other students were the ones who should have used it, not the teacher. Second, ignoring can be very subtle. If a student is so involved in disruption that he or she does not realize he or she is being ignored, disruption will not decrease and ignoring should not be used. In the second example, the teacher withdrew attention from the student when she isolated herself, but gave the student attention when she played with other students. The behavior of the target student was thus affected positively.

TIPS FOR IMPLEMENTATION

1. Identify the student and the target behavior.

2. Identify whose attention the student is seeking; that person should implement the ignoring intervention.

3. Ignore the student when the target behavior occurs.

4. Praise the student when the target behavior does not occur.

5. Provide attention to the student when the target behavior does not occur.

6. Praise other students who do not engage in the targeted behavior.

7. Turn away from the student when the target behavior occurs.

8. Evaluate the effectiveness of the intervention.

Sabatino (1983) suggested that teachers must exercise caution in choosing ignoring as an intervention. Teachers must first determine if the target behavior is one that indeed can be ignored. For example, common classroom behaviors, such as tattling, crying, whining, and interrupting, could be ignored provided they do not interfere with instruction. However, if the behavior is interfering with instruction or poses a threat to the student, teacher, or other students, then ignoring is obviously not the appropriate intervention. Sabatino stated that advantages of ignoring include its unobtrusive nature and the teacher's ability to implement the intervention concurrent with instruction.

Evertson, Emmer, Clements, Sanford, and Worsham (1984) maintained that ignoring is an appropriate intervention if the target behavior is a minor infraction. They also suggested that, if the target behavior is unlikely to

persist and speaking to the student would interfere with teaching, ignoring is a logical choice.

Bacon (1990), on the other hand, warned that "when the behavior fails to gain the desired attention, the behavior will eventually stop. Before the behavior stops, it may escalate to an unpleasant level in an attempt to demand teacher attention" (p. 608). The key here, of course, is to continue implementing the ignoring intervention, recognizing that the target behavior will probably decrease and stop once the student realizes that the teacher is not going to provide attention.

✔ **RESEARCH TO PRACTICE.** Systematic withdrawal of attention can be implemented easily by teachers once they are sure it is their attention that students are seeking (Sabatino, 1983). For instance, the example provided above of Debra and Ms. Chavez was drawn from a classic research experiment (Allen, Hart, Buell, Harris, & Wolf, 1964) and demonstrates the power of ignoring when it is systematically and consistently used. Ignoring is effective when the "desired" person withholds attention for undesirable performance. This is the reason why ignoring by a teacher seems to work best with younger students. To these students, adults' attention is very important. However, as students grow older, the attention of peers gains in importance. Although the value of a teacher's attention, support, and recognition should never be underestimated, a subtle tactic such as ignoring by an adult may lose power by the middle school grades. Thus, if the target student desires peer group attention, then the peer group must be taught to withhold attention. Research indicates that students also can use ignoring successfully. For example, Lovitt, Lovitt, Eaton, and Kirkwood (1973) found that, when a student consistently ignored his disruptive peer, classroom disturbance was reduced substantially.

Another important aspect of the Debra and Ms. Chavez example is that the teacher combined praise (and her attention) with ignoring. She gave attention to Debra when she engaged in the desired behavior and withheld it when she did not. In many situations, the results seem to be even stronger when specific praise and ignoring are paired.

PRACTICE WHAT YOU'VE LEARNED

1. Describe examples of classroom behaviors in which ignoring would be an (a) appropriate and (b) inappropriate intervention choice.

2. Describe ways to determine whose attention is being sought from the targeted student. This is an important factor because that person is the one who should do the ignoring.

3. Target a student for whom ignoring might be effective in changing an inappropriate behavior. Identify the inappropriate behavior, conduct baseline, identify when ignoring will be used and by whom, implement the ignoring intervention, and evaluate the effectiveness of the program.

4. Describe ways that body language (nonverbal communication) can be used as part of the ignoring intervention.

5. Identify when and how ignoring can be used as a schoolwide intervention.

6. Describe target behaviors for which specific praise paired with ignoring would be effective interventions.

7. Describe ways to teach secondary-level students to ignore the target student.

RULES

DEFINITION

Rules provide a code of conduct and expectations for all to follow.

Rules are a necessary part of society. They provide parameters and predictability to regulate behavior. Without rules, individuals are left to devise their own guidelines for creating consistency, predictability, and optimally some sense of security in their world (Windell, 1991).

DISCUSSION QUESTIONS

1. What are some rules of society by which we all must abide?

2. What experiences with rules do students bring to the classroom?

3. How do rules promote predictability and security for adults and children?

Students need rules of conduct and expectations, although these rules may vary somewhat across classroom settings. Teachers and administrators as a schoolwide unit need rules to manage student behavior and create a safe environment in which learning can occur. The location of rules on the Intervention Ladder is intentional: Most students will respond to rules, and some teacher time is necessary to discuss, implement, and enforce rules as an intervention. The importance of rules is illustrated in the following vignettes.

Mr. Bryant reminded several students that respecting other people's property was a rule of the class. Now they would have to decide how to repair the damaged game board that had been brought to class by a peer to be included in a cooperative learning activity.

After the bell rang, several students entered Mr. Taylor's class without offering an excuse or tardy slip. Not only were they late and noisy, but one student discovered that she had forgotten her textbook and left the class to go to her locker. Mr. Taylor began class even though several students were still standing in the back of the room talking. Other students were quiet and ready for the lesson to begin.

In Ms. Caldwell's class, students were permitted to enter the classroom in the morning before the bell rang to deposit backpacks and lunchboxes neatly by their desks. When the morning bell rang, students lined up by the classroom door where Ms. Caldwell stood waiting to greet them.

Several students had completed their independent work. They proceeded to a learning center to practice skills that had been taught in reading group the previous week. Their teacher, Mr. Schilit, worked with a math group and then checked with the students in the learning center to see if there were any questions.

Ms. Babkie reminded a student from another teacher's class that all students were expected to walk rather than run in the hall. She told the student that safety was very important and that walking would prevent an accident.

Several aspects about rules are noted in these vignettes. First, rules must be established for general classroom procedures. For example, in Mr. Bryant's class, "respecting other people's property" was a general rule applicable across any situation and activity. The Taylor vignette illustrates the need for a general rule—that is, be in your seats when the bell rings—that would have dealt with the tardy problem and the students standing in the back of the room even though it was time for class to begin. On the other hand, students in Ms. Caldwell's class knew the procedures for entering the classroom in the morning and storing their belongings (i.e., neatly).

Second, specific classroom procedural rules must be delineated. In the Schilit example, students moved to another classroom activity after their work was completed. Rather than interrupting the group lesson, the students realized that they had other activities to complete and that the teacher would check with them when he was able. Other examples of rules for specific activities might include rules for small-group work (e.g., "You may talk softly in your group," "You may move about the classroom to get materials

if needed"), rules for discussions (e.g., "Wait your turn to speak rather than raising your hand"), and rules for attending assemblies or plays (e.g., "Line up quietly, and remain quiet during the performance").

Third, schoolwide rules must be established and enforced by all teachers and administrators. As seen in the example above, Ms. Babkie reminded a student about a schoolwide rule even though that student was not in her class. Students must know that there is a set of rules for everyone in the school to follow and that enforcement will be carried out by all staff members.

DISCUSSION QUESTIONS

1. What are examples of general classroom rules that remain constant?

2. What are examples of specific classroom rules that pertain to activities or classroom situations?

3. What are examples of effective schoolwide rules? Ineffective rules?

Guidelines for Rules

GENERATE A LIST. Experience and reason provide us with some parameters about rules and how they are best delineated. To avoid the appearance of a repressive environment, the list of rules should not be extraordinarily long. The rules should be broad and fairly general so that a few rules encompass many situations. For example, rather than listing individual behaviors ("Don't talk out of turn"; "Don't sharpen your pencil"; "Don't sing in class"; "Don't get out of your seat without permission"; "Don't interrupt the teacher when he is working with an individual or group of students"), stating a general rule that encompasses many infractions is preferable (e.g., "Work quietly so you do not disturb your classmates"). When possible, it is also best to state rules positively rather than listing rules that exclusively indicate what not to do.

INVOLVE STUDENTS. Many teachers, counselors, and principals who have used rules in their school settings recommend that students be active participants in establishing those rules. Frequently, they suggest that at least one group discussion session be held during or soon after the first week at school, when students have enough experiences or incidents to discuss. One purpose of this session is to discuss their learning environment and how it can be improved. Therefore, they should be able to talk about those class occurrences that disturb their learning situation. This involvement in discussions about what makes an environment conducive to learning and what events distract from that climate can be an enriching growth experience for the students. Furthermore, it is important for the teacher to participate in these discussions and indicate to the students what behaviors he or she finds bothersome and, therefore, impair his or her ability to teach effectively.

Long and Frye (1977) suggested that, in group discussions for establishing rules, the teacher or counselor could do the following:

1. Ask general questions, such as "What do you consider to be appropriate and inappropriate classroom behaviors?"

2. Encourage group participation.

3. Ask specific questions, such as "Why do you feel that interrupting the teacher is not appropriate?"

4. Encourage divergent points of view.

5. Lead the class in establishing the rules of conduct for the class.

PROMOTE UNDERSTANDING. It is important that students understand what they are allowed to do, as well as what they are not allowed to do. Some teachers, during the rule development session, use the opportunity to indicate appropriate alternatives to rule infractions. For example, it is just as important to know when to sharpen pencils (before class begins) as it is to know when not to sharpen pencils (during the middle of an English or history lecture). In addition, many teachers use this opportunity to specify the consequences of breaking a rule. For example, sharpening pencils at the wrong time will result in the removal of that student's pencils for the remainder of the period. Any work not completed in class will have to be done as homework. After various rules are delineated and implemented, students should be allowed to monitor and review them periodically. As time goes on, some rules might become unnecessary and others might need to be developed. Rules should not be stagnant, but should change as the situation demands.

Besides rules that apply to specific classroom situations, rules applicable in schoolwide situations should be clear to all. This is particularly important at the middle and secondary levels. Campuswide rules might cover such areas as littering; defacement of school property; drugs or alcoholic beverages on campus; designated areas for food and beverages; smoking; and times for using the library, gym, and playground. The student council and school administrators might develop or revise these campuswide rules annually. The rules should then be distributed to the entire student body (maybe in the form of a handbook), and teachers should ensure that the rules are read and understood by all school members. As with classroom rules, students should be allowed to have input regarding campuswide regulations. A process for modifications should be developed, perhaps one in which suggestions are channeled through elected student representatives. Some principals and counselors take this opportunity to delineate the ways in which these rules will be enforced, so the expectations and the results of infractions are clear to all.

PROVIDE REMINDERS.   Sabatino (1983) described the procedure of rule reminders. Because certain situations may provoke inappropriate behavior (i.e., rule breaking), the astute teacher will recognize these times and remind students about the rules. For instance, if students are lining up to go to the library, a reminder about walking quietly in the halls may be in order. Or, if the bell will ring in a minute, the teacher might remind students about the need to be in their seats when the bell rings. Teachers can also ask questions about a certain rule so that the students verbalize it rather than the teacher taking this responsibility. For example, when returning from physical education, the teacher may ask students the rule about entering the classroom (i.e., quietly).

TIPS FOR IMPLEMENTATION

1. Decide what code of conduct and expectations must be in place in the classroom.

2. Discuss ideas for rules with students.

3. Determine no more than seven rules that can be followed and understood by all.

4. Phrase rules in the positive as much as possible.

5. Identify positive consequences for rule observance.

6. Identify logical negative consequences for infractions.

7. Enforce the rules and apply the consequences consistently.

8. Inform parents and administrators about classroom rules and consequences.

9. Teach the rules.

10. Remind students about the rules.

11. Praise students for following the rules.

12. As circumstances change, revise rules accordingly.

13. Be sure the rules are age appropriate.

Problems Associated with Rules

Sometimes, problems arise in classrooms and schools that are related to rules. For example, students do not behave according to adult expectations because they do not understand what is expected of them. Educators often assume that students know how they are supposed to act in school settings, but this assumption is faulty for several reasons. First, despite the frequency with which school personnel imply the guidelines of school conduct, the codes are often not delineated clearly. Students do not fully understand the meaning of these codes. In some school situations, they learn about the standards of behavior by accident, or learn about the existence of a rule when they break it and are punished for that infraction. This can result in incomplete knowledge of school and classroom codes. Although most students will eventually come to understand these unstated expectations, a trial-and-error process is not efficient and requires a number of infractions before full understanding is achieved. Clearly, the explicit statement of rules of conduct and expectations helps to alleviate the need for trial-and-error learning.

The second reason why many students do not come to school with an intuitive knowledge of behavioral expectations rests with educators themselves. Educators are individuals with different tolerances for various behaviors (e.g., noise, freedom of movement), and are therefore inconsistent as a group in their expectations of students. During the school day, students are required to act appropriately with a substantial number of different adults, all with individual styles and tolerances. At the secondary level, students may interact with six or seven different teachers each day, whereas at the elementary level, students may have one primary teacher and several other teachers for therapy, fine arts, and physical education. These discrepancies in styles confuse many students who do not possess the discrimination skills necessary to make adjustments to diverse settings requiring subtle differences in behavior. In addition to not being able to discriminate the behavioral repertoires expected from different teachers, students must also know how to respond in different school situations. For example, the response demands in physical education are different from those in history class, drama, and study hall. When the conduct of students indicates that they are not certain of the behavior demanded by the setting, teachers must establish rules that clearly specify what is expected.

A third reason why problems arise is that the rules may not be age appropriate. For instance, expecting kindergarten students at the beginning of the year to stand quietly in line without touching their neighbors may not be realistic. By the same token, a rule for senior high students to keep their hands and feet to themselves probably will not be well received. (The topic of fighting may be discussed at some point during the year, but a rule about hands and feet might be perceived as "babyish" and thus resented.)

✔ **RESEARCH TO PRACTICE.** Most schools and teachers have rules. As a vehicle to clarify schoolwide and general classroom codes of expected behavior, one school district developed a behavior checklist for its middle school students (see Table 3.1) that provides a detailed list of behaviors expected at school. After studying and discussing these "rules," students and school personnel should understand the behavioral norms. Such detailed checklists might be helpful when more general sets of school and classroom rules are ineffective.

In some school settings, the detailing of rules is not necessary. However, in settings where discipline is viewed as a problem, guidelines for deportment might eliminate the need for more drastic interventions. Once they are delineated, discussed, and understood, the parameters of school expectations are no longer elusive. Infractions should lead to intervention, and living within those parameters should result in a more positive learning environment.

PRACTICE WHAT YOU'VE LEARNED

1. Brainstorm examples of positive rules, such as "Follow directions."

2. Identify examples of rules that are negatively worded and try to rephrase them in the positive, such as "No talking" could be changed to "Raise your hand to speak."

3. Brainstorm examples of positive schoolwide rules, such as "Walk in the halls."

4. Discuss positive and negative consequences for rules. Remember that consequences must be enforceable.

5. Discuss general and specific rules, that is, rules that generally apply all of the time regardless of the type of instructional format or location, and rules that apply to specific activities, such as small-group work, lining up, or learning centers.

6. Describe ways to teach rules and to remind students about rules.

7. Identify other interventions from the Intervention Ladder that could be paired with rules to promote effective discipline in the classroom.

TABLE 3.1
Behavioral Checklist

Student's Name _____ Grade _____ Date _____

Homeroom Teacher _____

Check boxes that best describe behaviors

Behaviors	Meets Standards	Below Standards	Rarely Shown	Comments
Building-related:				
1. Walks in halls				
2. Walks in halls quietly				
3. Has pass when in hall				
4. Is not disruptive				
5. Arrives at classes on time				
6. Interacts with adults properly				
7. Leaves building appropriately				
Schedule-related:				
1. Attends regularly				
2. Checks in when late or absent				
3. Attends class on time				
4. Attends school on time				
Classroom-related:				
1. Sits at desk				
2. Raises hand				
3. Enters room quietly				
4. Interacts appropriately with peers				
5. Has required materials & supplies				
6. Has assignments completed on time				
7. Able to deal with criticism well				
8. Meets teacher's behaviorial expectations				
9. Participates appropriately in classroom discussions				
10. Takes notes				
11. Asks for help appropriately				
12. Leaves room appropriately				

CONTINGENT INSTRUCTIONS

DEFINITION

Contingent instructions means that, after an occurrence of the target behavior, the teacher quietly and on a one-to-one basis tells the individual specifically not to engage in that activity.

Students must understand what is expected of them in school environments. Rules, in part, help to clarify the standards of expected deportment. As discussed in the previous section, rules must not seem to be overbearing, too stringent, or excessive in length. As all who work in school settings know, even with a set of agreed-upon rules, disruption will occur. There are at least three reasons for this:

1. The students did not understand the implications of the rules.

2. They forgot what the rules are.

3. They purposely defied those rules.

Whatever the reason, when a rule is broken, there must be a consequence. For most minor, infrequent infractions, the consequence should be minor. Before any complicated intervention technique is used, a simple tactic should be tried. Contingent instructions are logical tactics to use first in many such situations. The following vignette exemplifies how and when contingent instructions can be used successfully.

Ms. Scott had established classroom rules with her students at the beginning of the year. Initially, the rules were reviewed at the beginning of each period to help students remember the expectations in the classroom. Ms. Scott used reinforcement and specific praise when rules were followed and instituted consequences for rules that were broken. Jon was working on the rule, "Raise your hand to speak." He tended to call out answers rather than raise his hand. Ms. Scott tried specific praise when Jon remembered to raise his hand and ignored him when he called out. Ms. Scott recorded occurrences of Jon's calling out behavior and decided that specific praise and ignoring were not producing the results she sought: reducing and then eliminating the target behavior. She implemented contingent instructions. Each time Jon called out rather than raised his hand to speak, she walked to his desk and quietly reminded him about the rule. She then immediately called on another student to answer the question.

As with praise and the other intervention tactics discussed in this chapter, instructions given to reduce disruption should be specific and directly relevant to the target behavior. Contingent instructions, which are very useful in these situations, should be delivered *after* an occurrence of the target behavior. They should specifically address the infraction and be presented as privately as possible once eye contact has been established (Van Houten, Nau, MacKenzie-Keating, Sameoto, & Colavecchia, 1982). Maurer (1988) pointed out that teachers should use three nonverbal behaviors when reprimanding students for inappropriate actions or breaking the rules. First, the teacher should establish eye contact. Second, the teacher should be two to three feet from the student so that a strong physical teacher presence is evident but not intrusive on the student's space. Third, the teacher's voice intensity should remain calm and the pitch average. Loud talking, which calls attention to the teacher–student interaction, weakens the effectiveness of the intervention.

TIPS FOR IMPLEMENTATION

1. Try specific praise and ignoring first.

2. Implement contingent instructions after the target behavior occurs.

3. Establish eye contact.

4. Provide specific information about the rule that is broken or the inappropriate behavior that must be stopped.

5. Talk quietly and privately to the student; avoid calling across the room to the student.

6. Praise the student when the appropriate behavior occurs.

✔ **RESEARCH TO PRACTICE.** Although few examples of the use of contingent instructions appear in the research literature, those that are available are very helpful. In one study (Roberts & Smith, 1977), contingent instructions successfully reduced two preschoolers' frequency of physical aggression. One student, John, was extremely aggressive, and his teachers were concerned for the other students' safety. John's aggression comprised the following behaviors: pulling hair, kicking, hitting, pushing, pinching, knocking down others, bearhugging, throwing, biting, grabbing, and pulling. The initial data indicated that John's incidences of aggression averaged almost 20 per day, within a 30-minute period of free play. The procedures that operated initially (baseline) were ignoring John for his aggressions and attending to the victim. This procedure did not reduce the number of John's aggressive acts, and another tactic had to be implemented. In another phase of the study, the experimenter came to John after each aggression and instructed him not to engage in that action. For example, if John hit another student, the experimenter said to him "Don't hit" immediately following the act. As Figure 3.1 shows, this intervention successfully reduced the target behavior. However, there was some question from the other teachers about whether John's behavior improved as a result of the instructions or as a result of the nonverbal features of the intervention—that is, *how* the experimenter delivered the instructions. Therefore, the *non sequitur* condition was scheduled in which the experimenter acted as he had previously but said to the student "Birds fly" rather than "Don't hit" or some other specific contingent instruction. The number of acts of aggression began to rise at an alarming rate, and the contingent instructions were rescheduled successfully.

In another study (O'Leary, Kaufman, Kass, & Drabman, 1970), the influences of loud and soft reprimands were compared. Amounts of classroom noise and disruption were substantially reduced when the teacher went to a disruptive student and quietly reprimanded her; however, when the reprimand was audible to the class, disruption did not fall to desirable levels. Baron (1988) found that individuals resist changing their behavior if criticism is not delivered in a manner showing consideration for the individual. This research further supports the notion that instructions given for appropriate behavior are more effective if delivered privately to the student.

Summary of Studies

Contingent instructions can be used effectively when

1. They are specific.

2. They immediately follow the target behavior.

3. They do not draw class attention to either the behavior or the offender.

Although contingent instructions will not help all students reach a desired level of conduct, teachers can try implementing the strategy early, before the other interventions found higher on the Intervention Ladder.

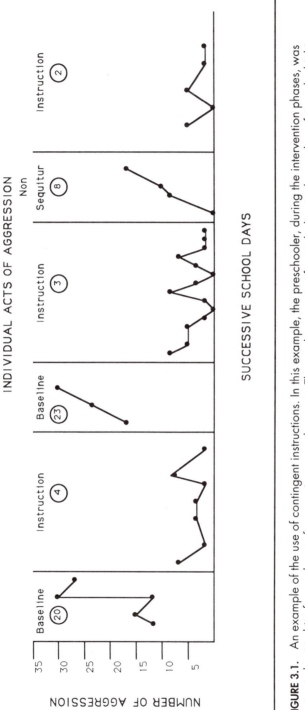

FIGURE 3.1. An example of the use of contingent instructions. In this example, the preschooler, during the intervention phases, was instructed not to hit after each act of aggression on a classmate. The result was a significant decline in the number of times he hit his peers during recess.

PRACTICE WHAT YOU'VE LEARNED

1. Describe ways that contingent instructions can be used as part of a schoolwide discipline program.

2. Identify a student for whom contingent instructions would be an appropriate intervention. Describe the target behavior, collect baseline, implement the intervention, collect data, and evaluate the effectiveness of the intervention.

3. Describe how contingent instructions can be used in secondary-level classes.

4. Describe how contingent instructions can be used in elementary-level classes.

CONTINGENT OBSERVATION

DEFINITION

Contingent observation means that a disruptive student is removed from a group activity, but still allowed to observe the proceedings.

Contingent observation is a form of timeout (Gast & Nelson, 1977a, 1977b), which implies the removal of an individual from a reinforcing situation. In this intervention, a student who is acting inappropriately is isolated from the group activity, but can still watch the activity from a removed vantage point. The benefits of this type of timeout are that the student does not lose valuable instruction time and that he or she is still in a position to watch peers model the expected social and academic behaviors. The following descriptions represent an example and a nonexample of contingent observation timeout.

Bob was not paying attention to his teacher and was playing with the science equipment during an experiment. Mr. Cantrell asked Bob to leave the science table and watch the experiment from one of the desks toward the back of the room. Bob did as requested, but after 5 minutes became disruptive again.

Ms. Smiley asked Samuel to take his chair and sit away from the group because he could not keep his hands to himself during the dinosaur activities. Ms. Smiley told Samuel that he had to leave the group because he could not keep his hands to himself and that he must sit quietly for 3 minutes before he could join the group again. She set the timer for 3 minutes. Ms. Smiley and the other students continued to work on constructing graphs about dinosaurs and creating dioramas. After 3 minutes of sitting quietly, Samuel was allowed to rejoin the group with a private reminder to keep his hands to himself if he wanted to continue with his activity.

In the nonexample of contingent observation, Mr. Cantrell correctly applied the procedure by having Bob, the disruptive student, leave the group activity. This action was justified because neither Bob nor his classmates could benefit from the planned experience due to his bothersome behavior. However, after being away from the group and the teacher's control for a while, his interest in the group activity waned. Because of his exclusion, he again became bothersome. If he had been allowed to rejoin the activity after several minutes of contingent observation timeout, the reoccurrence of the disruptive behavior would most likely have been avoided.

In the example of contingent observation, Ms. Smiley correctly applied the contingent observation intervention by (a) identifying the behavior that was inappropriate, (b) telling the student what he had done that was unacceptable, (c) removing him from a group activity that he enjoyed, (d) telling him the time limit that acceptable behavior must occur while he was removed from the group, (e) working with the other students and ignoring Samuel, (f) asking Samuel to rejoin the group after his time was up and he had sat quietly, and (g) reminding him privately about the expected appropriate behavior for continued participation. Ms. Smiley also set a timer for 3 minutes, which is an appropriate method to use with younger students.

TIPS FOR IMPLEMENTATION

1. Identify the student's inappropriate behavior.

2. Provide a warning for the occurrence of the inappropriate behavior, informing the student that the next occurrence of the behavior will be followed by isolation from the group.

3. Remove the student if the inappropriate behavior occurs again, and briefly explain why the student is being removed and how long isolation will occur.

4. Set a short time for the student's isolation from the group, and state that rejoining the group is contingent on sitting quietly for a specified time.

5. Ignore the student during isolation time.

6. Be sure that the student wants to be involved in the group activity.

7. Provide a quiet reminder of the appropriate behavior when the student rejoins the group.

DISCUSSION QUESTIONS

1. For what behaviors at the preschool, elementary, and secondary levels would contingent observation be effective?

2. What are some cautions about using contingent observation?

3. When would contingent observation not be effective at the secondary level?

4. What other interventions could be paired with contingent observation?

5. How could contingent observation work with ignoring, specific praise, and rules?

CRITERION-SPECIFIC REWARDS

DEFINITION

Criterion-specific rewards means that the student earns a special privilege only for reaching the desired level of the target behavior.

Teachers can encourage discipline and improved school performance through the careful use of various reinforcement procedures. Although most educators are aware of the power that reinforcement has on school behaviors, these systems are sometimes not used because of teachers' reluctance to reward students for expected behavior. Another reason teachers do not use rewards is their past experience with inefficient or costly reinforcement systems.

DISCUSSION QUESTIONS

1. What is your philosophy about rewarding students for appropriate behavior?

2. What experiences have you had with reinforcement systems?

3. What are examples of reinforcers that are part of daily life?

Educators often express concerns about rewarding students who act appropriately. These concerns are discussed below, along with possible recommendations for addressing each one.

Rewarding Appropriate Behavior

The first concern—reluctance to reward students for expected behavior—is real and reflects a philosophical point of view about the ideal school situation. Should students be rewarded for merely meeting normal expectations? If preventive measures and those tactics found lower on the Intervention Ladder—praise, ignoring, rules, and contingent instructions—have proven unsuccessful, many of the options left are punitive in nature. The widespread use of punitive measures could seriously alter the learning environment, a choice that is not desirable.

Rewarding students for not disrupting the learning environment is a positive option and most often successful. If reinforcement is used to reduce disruption, it should be used to improve other school performance as well. If the only opportunity to receive rewards is by misbehaving, soon many students might misbehave to earn rewards. In a reward system, all good conduct should be rewarded whether or not the students have been offenders in the past. Even those who never disrupt or violate school and classroom rules should have the opportunity to earn rewards; this might be arranged by providing special rewards for outstanding academic achievement or improved grades. However it is organized, the reward system should recognize all those with good conduct, not only the potential "troublemakers" who have exhibited appropriate behaviors.

Thus, when setting up a rewards system, educators might utilize the following suggestions:

1. Identify appropriate behavior.

2. Establish criterion for appropriate behavior.

3. Identify students, intermittently, who are acting appropriately.

4. Reward the students individually or as a group only if rewards are earned.

Selecting Reasonable Rewards

The second reason for not using reinforcement procedures—past experience with inefficient and costly systems—needs to be discounted. Rewards offered students need not be expensive, tangible, or complicated. Tangible reinforcement items not only are costly, but in many cases are unnecessary. Overall point or "token" systems are not always required or necessarily desirable. The system for earning rewards need not be complicated. Simple systems can be more effective than complex ones. The general rule of thumb is to keep teaching as simple as possible.

Identifying Appropriate Rewards/Reinforcers

Educators often are concerned about what rewards or reinforcers will work most effectively with students. Teachers may spend time searching for ideal reinforcers, only to find that they do not serve the purpose when presented to students. This rather simple problem can be corrected easily, as demonstrated in the following research.

✔ **RESEARCH TO PRACTICE.** Raschke, Stainback, and Stainback (1982) compared the predictive capabilities of parents, teachers, and students in selecting appropriate rewards. The results indicated that there is often a significant discrepancy between the reward preferences of pupils and the rewards actually used by educators. According to the results of this study, the only group that can accurately predict the potential influence of an anticipated reinforcer (reward) for educational tasks is the students themselves. Although teachers and parents think they know what reinforces student behavior, apparently they do not. Because the key to the effective use of reinforcement systems is the selection of the reinforcers, it is imperative that students be active participants in the selection process. The rewards must be highly desirable to the individuals working to earn them. This means that they might best be individually determined. The fourth graders might want to earn extra library time, but eighth graders might desire more time to work on a science project.

In an informal survey we conducted, students at the elementary and secondary levels indicated their preferences for rewards. These preferences are found in Table 3.2. Other examples of rewards for secondary students include (a) grades, (b) certificates of recognition, (c) honor roll club recognition at the end of each grading period, (d) bulletin board decoration, and (e) age-appropriate board games (Emmer, Evertson, Sanford, Clements, & Worsham, 1984), (f) library pass, (g) choice of seat, and (h) no homework (Hall & Hall, 1980). For elementary students, rewards might be (a) happy faces, (b) stars, (c) stickers, (d) student of the week, (e) super stars, (f) good work displayed on bulletin board, (g) puzzles and games (Evertson et al., 1984), (h) choice of playground equipment, (i) assignment reduction, and (j) principal's helper (Hall & Hall, 1980).

TABLE 3.2
Rewards Suggested by Students

Working with a friend in the hall	Obtaining legal hall passes
Collecting the lunch money	Running errands for the teacher
Taking attendance	Taking notes to other teachers
Taking the attendance cards to the office	Taking good work to the principal or counselor
Running off dittos and collating papers	Free time for special projects
Early dismissal	Extra recess
Writing something on a ditto master and running it off	Sticker on a behavioral report card
Sitting at the teacher's desk to do the assigned seatwork	Lunchtime basketball games, with the teacher serving as referee
Viewing noneducational videotapes on Friday afternoon	Popcorn during educational films
Extra shop or P.E. time	Special parties
Special picnic lunches or food treats	Field trips
More assemblies	Special art projects
Working on games or puzzles	Listening to the radio
Typing on a typewriter	Decorating the bulletin board
Extra library time	Being a group leader
Helping the class line up at the door	Leading the class to the library
Reading a magazine	Lunch with the teacher
Listening to a tape with headphones	Note home to the parents
Working on the computer	Watering the plants
Feeding the class animals	No homework pass for one night
Sitting next to a friend	Going to another classroom as a cross-age tutor

These guidelines are presented for preparing to use reinforcers/rewards:

1. Observe students and determine what activities they prefer.

2. Ask students what activities or privileges they would like to earn.

3. Conduct a survey to determine preferences.

4. Have a variety of age-appropriate options.

5. Be prepared to change the options as student preferences change.

6. Be sure the reinforcers are reasonable, that is, inexpensive, easy to locate and implement in the classroom setting, and enjoyable by students in a short amount of class time.

7. Encourage students to suggest activities they would like to earn time to do.

8. Plan on time in the daily or weekly schedule for students to enjoy their earned reinforcers.

DISCUSSION QUESTIONS

1. What reinforcers have worked effectively for you at the elementary level?

2. What reinforcers have worked effectively for you at the secondary level?

3. How did you determine what reinforcers to have available?

4. How frequently did you have to change reinforcers?

Establishing a Reinforcement Schedule

In addition to selecting reinforcers, establishing criterion for earning reinforcers, and preparing for reinforcement procedures in the classroom, teachers need to consider schedules of reinforcement, which are important because of the individual needs of students. For example, some students require immediate reinforcement contingent on achieving the specified criterion for performance, whereas other students require reinforcement on an intermittent, unpredictable basis to maintain the criterion level. Because of the concern for identifying and establishing an appropriate reinforcement schedule to match the needs of various students, we discuss below some of the types of reinforcement schedules and when their use is appropriate.

In a thorough review of reducing misbehavior through reinforcement, Deitz and Repp (1983) described different types of reinforcement schedules. Although several of these schedules are somewhat complicated, the most difficult aspects of these procedures are their names. In the differential reinforcement of behavior omission (DRO), a reward is given if the behavior does not occur for a certain period of time (for a thorough review of DRO, see Poling and Ryan, 1982). In other words, if Maria acts appropriately during art period, she will earn the opportunity to listen to the school orchestra rehearse. For some situations, the required unit of time of good behavior needs to be shorter than one academic period.

Two schedules of reinforcement also used to reduce misbehavior are differential reinforcement of incompatible behavior (DRI) and differential reinforcement of alternative behaviors (DRA). In the DRI situation, the student is reinforced when he or she engages in a behavior that is incompatible with the unwanted one. For example, Eloy cannot be in his seat and out of his seat at the same time. He could be rewarded for being in his seat for a longer period of time, thus reducing his "out-of-seat" time. In the DRA situation, the student is rewarded for a constructive behavior that is not necessarily incompatible with the undesirable one. For example, Sharon can talk out of turn and still complete seatwork assignments, but if she is rewarded for completing more assignments, she should have less time to talk out.

Another reinforcement schedule that has great appeal is differential reinforcement of low rates of responding (DRL) (Deitz & Repp, 1973). In this situation, rewards are given only when the amount of undesired behavior falls below a preestablished criterion, as in the following example.

> Patrice was unruly on the school bus. The bus driver, Ms. Gonzales, was distracted because of Patrice's excessive noise, swearing, and mobility. She counted the number of these behavioral incidents for several mornings and found that Patrice typically engaged in 15 distracting behaviors on each morning's bus ride. Ms. Gonzales arranged a DRL for Patrice. She told her that if she acted inappropriately no more than five times on the morning bus ride, she could choose her seat for the next day. If she acted out even less, three or four times, she could be the first person off the bus that morning. If she acted inappropriately only one or two times, she could both choose her seat and be the first one off the bus. If she stayed in her seat, did not swear, or make noise, in addition to the two other rewards, a good note would be sent to her homeroom teacher.

This application of the DRL procedure has several nice features. First, the goal for the expected bus riding behavior was set and explained. Patrice did not receive reinforcement for any amount of improved performance; considerable effort had to be made to achieve the goal. The amount of reward increased as Patrice came closer to achieving the expected behavior of no distractions on her bus ride.

Selecting and Implementing a Reinforcement Schedule

The following list should help teachers establish a reinforcement schedule.

1. Select the behavior to be changed (target behavior).

2. Specify a criterion level for acceptable performance.

3. Select the appropriate schedule of reinforcement.

4. Determine when the reinforcer will be given.

5. Have the student identify a reinforcer.

6. Implement and evaluate the program.

PRACTICE WHAT YOU'VE LEARNED

1. Identify classroom target behaviors for a reinforcement program.

2. Identify schoolwide target behaviors for a reinforcement program.

3. Discuss ways to acquaint students with a reinforcement program.

4. Discuss examples of target behaviors for each type of reinforcement schedule.

FINES

DEFINITION

A *fine* is the loss of privileges by a student after engaging in the target behavior.

As discussed in the previous section, one way to achieve discipline and maintain a positive school environment is to allow students to earn privileges for good or improved behavior. However, privileges can be withheld when students do not perform up to the standards of acceptable behavior (Polsgrove & Rieth, 1983). Fines can be implemented either in conjunction with earning privileges or against privileges that are received merely because students attend school. Elsewhere in the literature, the intervention of fines also is referred to as response cost (e.g., Alberto & Troutman, 1990; Walker, 1983). An example of withholding privileges is described below.

> A class was allowed to earn a free period each week when all of their homework assignments were turned in daily and they entered the class without disruption each period change. One day, the teacher was ill and a substitute teacher replaced her. Unfortunately, the class was not cooperative with the substitute. They were excessively noisy, refused to do the assignments she gave them, and in several instances were rude to her. Although the class had met the criterion for earning a free period that week, the class was fined because of their misconduct with the substitute. They did not receive the free period that week.

In this example, the earning and the losing of a privilege were connected. The students could not receive a privilege if they misbehaved in another specified situation. Of course, under this system, all students should be aware of those behaviors that both earn and lose privileges. If fines are used, they should not be determined at the moment of the infraction. With some careful thought, those behaviors that earn privileges can be clearly delineated, along with those that result in fines in the form of loss of privileges.

In typical school situations, students are given many privileges without earning them. For example, movies, sporting events, field trips, assemblies, and many other activities are provided regardless of deportment. Many consider participation in such events as their inalienable right. However, all students also have the right to learn and study in a school atmosphere that is free from disruption. Those students who infringe on the rights of their classmates possibly should lose the opportunity to participate in a special event. In other words, those who break serious school rules could be fined for their misconduct. That fine might result in their not being able to participate in a special school event. The following is a description of an unfortunate situation in which fines were used.

> The time for changing periods became very disorderly at one middle school. Books were thrown in the halls, students shouted at one another or occasionally fought with each other, and the noise level far surpassed any acceptable level. The school counselor decided to implement a fine system. He and several monitors stood in the halls during period changes and passed out cards to those who were disorderly. Anyone receiving a card could not attend that week's assembly. Unfortunately, the number receiving cards each day rose substantially due to the content of the

assemblies. The students thought that the assemblies were boring, did not want to attend them, and found a way to be excused.

In this example, fining for inappropriate behavior was unsuccessful for two reasons. First, the privilege lost for disruption during period changes was not a privilege that the students viewed as desirable. Second, because the privilege was lost with the receipt of only one card, there was nothing more to lose by additional fines. Thus, those who had already been fined had little reason not to engage in even more disruption. The obvious caution is to be sure that students want the particular privilege so that they will not purposefully be disruptive to be fined and thus lose the privilege. Also, teachers must be sure that a fining intervention system does not result in students losing all privileges early in the day or week and thus having no reason to behave appropriately.

Another method of fining is to give students point cards with a large number of points at the beginning of the day and to take away points all day for infractions. This method should be used with caution because it focuses on the negative aspects of behavior management and does not provide students with positive recognition for appropriate behavior. A final caution concerns the common practice for inappropriate behavior of having students write numerous times that they will not misbehave again. In this case, the students are losing the privilege of time, especially if sentences are written after school. The danger with this type of fine is that students could develop a dislike for the act of writing, which is certainly not something educators want to instill in students.

DISCUSSION QUESTIONS

1. What are some privileges secondary-level students can earn for appropriate behavior?

2. What are some privileges elementary-level students can earn for appropriate behavior?

3. What are some privileges secondary-level students receive simply because they attend school?

4. What are some privileges elementary-level students receive simply because they attend school?

5. Of the privileges that students can earn or receive based on attendance, which are likely targets for fines based on inappropriate behavior?

6. What are some cautions for using fines?

✔ **RESEARCH TO PRACTICE.** In a study of using fines to improve computational accuracy and reduce carelessness in responding, Lovitt and Smith (1974) fined a student a minute of recess for each incorrectly answered arithmetic problem. First, these researchers ascertained that the student could indeed solve the problems accurately; the mistakes were careless and purposive. Second, the researchers told the student that for each problem wrong she would lose a minute of recess. The student was praised for accuracy. Because recess was important to the student, her accuracy in arithmetic computation quickly improved to criterion.

TIPS FOR IMPLEMENTATION

1. Identify the target behavior.

2. Decide on the privilege that will be taken away (fined) based on the presence of the target behavior.

3. Determine how much of a privilege will be lost over what course of time.

4. Be sure students do not purposefully engage in the target behavior because they want to lose a certain privilege.

5. Tie the fine directly to the target behavior (e.g., if the target behavior is to reduce student talking during independent seatwork time, then the fine might be to lose the privilege of sitting next to a friend if the two cannot work quietly).

PRACTICE WHAT YOU'VE LEARNED

1. Design a hypothetical intervention plan using fines as the intervention. Be sure to include information from the Tips for Implementation section and the cautions presented above.

2. Discuss how fines can be used as part of a schoolwide discipline program.

3. Discuss ways to pair fines with a positive intervention, such as specific praise or criterion-specific rewards.

4. Identify the pros and cons of the fines intervention.

GROUP CONTINGENCIES

In the section about ignoring disruption as a procedure to eliminate it, we considered the importance of knowing whose attention the disruptive parties are seeking. As students grow older, attention from the peer group becomes increasingly important. Researchers (e.g., Salend, 1987; Salend & Lamb,

1986) have shown that the use of group contingencies is an effective intervention for managing student behavior.

Group contingency plans tap the peer group as a resource to encourage positive changes in performance. They also can add an element of fun to the school program. Litow and Pumroy (1975) provided the conceptual scheme for three different types of group contingencies: *dependent, independent,* and *interdependent.* Although they vary somewhat as to who earns and who receives the reward, they all involve students as a group of peers.

Dependent Group Contingency

DEFINITION

A *dependent group contingency* is one in which a person earns privileges or rewards for peers by behaving appropriately.

In a dependent group contingency, one student may earn privileges for an entire class or for a small group of classmates. For example, one person might earn the privilege of leaving for lunch several minutes early for the five students sitting around her by staying in her seat for the entire study hall period. When planned carefully, dependent group contingencies have several aspects that make them useful. A student who is not valued by her peers can earn privileges for them. This often increases that person's importance to the others. Those who plan the contingencies must be certain, however, that the target student is capable of performing the desired behavior and, thereby, can earn the rewards for the others. This is important, for if a situation is established in which the student cannot succeed, the group's regard for that student will deteriorate even further.

Another positive feature often results from this kind of arrangement: The peers become involved in the classmate's improvement. When this plan is in operation, those who benefit from the target student's good behavior often encourage their classmate by showing her what to do in the targeted situation, talking with her about it during breaks, and praising her when the reward is earned. Experience indicates that, if positive group action is to be achieved, the group should consist of individuals the target student values. Placing members of the school literary society around the center of the football team might not be the best arrangement. Regardless, with careful selection of the target student's behavior to be rewarded and the peer group to benefit from the improved performance, dependent group contingencies can have an overall positive effect that might not be achieved otherwise.

DISCUSSION QUESTIONS

1. What behaviors might be appropriate for a dependent group contingency?

2. What are ways to ensure that the student is capable of performing the target behavior?

3. How would this plan be explained to other students?

4. How would rewards be decided?

5. How would a reward schedule be determined?

TIPS FOR IMPLEMENTATION

1. Identify the student whose behavior needs to be changed.

2. Identify the target behavior.

3. Identify how frequently the target behavior is occurring before intervention.

4. Be sure the target behavior is one that the student can change under dependent group contingency conditions.

5. Identify the group of students who will benefit from the dependent group contingency plan.

6. Identify with the students what reward will be earned by all contingent on the target student's behavior.

7. Identify when the students will earn the reward.

8. Collect data on the effectiveness of the plan.

Independent Group Contingency

DEFINITION

An *independent group contingency* is one in which individuals earn reinforcement when they achieve a goal established for the group.

In independent group contingencies, individuals earn a reward once they meet an established group goal. As shown in the following vignette, when this system is in effect, each person in the group is rewarded as soon as he or she achieves the goal.

Ms. Voress could not get her class to remember to bring their homework assignments for social studies. Despite her constant reminders and threats of reduced grades, her students forgot to bring their homework to school. She explained to them that her goal was for all members of her class to complete and submit their homework assignments to her on the day they were due. Each pupil who met this goal would be excused from the following day's homework. Assignments turned in on time rose to nearly 100% for social studies.

One advantage of independent group contingencies is that the entire group is not denied the reward because of the forgetfulness of a few. In the dependent group contingency, the plan's success often depends on the students' abilities to achieve the reward. If the probability of that occurrence (e.g., all students remembering their homework) is low, the independent group contingency plan should be considered.

DISCUSSION QUESTIONS

1. What behaviors might be appropriate for an independent group contingency?

2. How would this plan be explained to students?

3. How would rewards be decided?

4. How would a reward schedule be determined?

TIPS FOR IMPLEMENTATION

1. Identify a target behavior that is appropriate for many of the students to achieve.

2. Establish criterion level for attainment of a reward.

3. Have students identify the reward.

4. Identify the reward schedule, that is, how often the reward will be given when criterion is reached.

5. Collect data to determine the success of the independent group contingency.

Interdependent Group Contingency

DEFINITION

An *interdependent group contingency* is one in which the class or group earns a special reward when the entire class meets the established goal.

Interdependent group contingency, the most common form of group contingency, has numerous versions, some of which are translated into games. In this arrangement, the entire group benefits or does not benefit from the actions of the group. Because an individual's behavior is often directly or indirectly encouraged by a group, this system has great appeal to many teachers, for all who participate in the inappropriate activity participate in its consequences. This form of group contingency is effective for all age groups. Therefore, students in kindergarten through 12th grade can benefit from this intervention. For example, in kindergarten, before a snack is distributed, all students must be sitting quietly in their chairs. For elementary-level students, an example of an interdependent group contingency might be that all students must have their desks in order before lunch dismissal. Secondary-level students could be expected to arrive on time to class for 3 days and thus earn no homework for one evening.

The following example of an application of interdependent group contingency was drawn from Sulzbacher and Houser (1968).

Ms. Houser was an elementary teacher. During the first few weeks of school, Ms. Houser's students realized that she became terribly embarrassed when any of them used or talked about the "naughty finger." Although not all of the students engaged in this behavior, it became clear to Ms. Houser and her consultant that all of her class was participating in the inappropriate behavior, at least indirectly, by laughing and encouraging the others. During the intervention period, Ms. Houser placed at the front of the classroom a flipchart with 11 cards ranging from 10 to 0. She explained to the class that at the end of each day there would be a 10-minute special recess. However, each time she saw or heard about the "naughty finger," she would flip over one card on the chart (to the next card and a lower number), and the special recess was reduced by 1 minute. Even on the first day, a substantial reduction in the undesirable behavior was noted.

DISCUSSION QUESTIONS

1. What behaviors probably indicated Ms. Houser's embarrassment with the naughty finger?

2. What is the target behavior in this example?

3. How does group behavior promote the occurrence of the target behavior?

4. How was special recess determined as the reward?

5. How is this an example of an interdependent group contingency?

6. How could data have been collected to determine the effectiveness of the contingency plan?

For social reasons, the system used in the example was very effective. First, the teacher's embarrassment was noticeable to all of the students; they enjoyed having control over her. With the system she devised, Ms. Houser did not have to discuss the situation with them, so the probability of their embarrassing her was reduced. Second, most of the class was directly or indirectly involved in the disruption. There were no longer any scapegoats; everyone participated in the loss and gain of the reward. Third, the data and evaluation system of the flipped cards indicated the number of inappropriate occurrences during the day. No additional actions were needed for evaluation. Finally, the teacher regained more instruction time than she had lost to the confusion and disruption that centered on the target behavior. Clearly, in the early stages of the study, the students wasted more time engaging in disruption than the teacher let them earn when the contingency (special recess) was scheduled.

✔ **RESEARCH TO PRACTICE.** *The Good Behavior Game,* developed by Barrish, Saunders, and Wolf (1969), uses class competition to reduce disruption. The class is divided into two teams. Whenever someone talks out or is out of seat, his or her team receives a point. At the end of the day, the team with the fewest points wins the game. If both teams score very few points, both teams win; if both teams have too many points, both lose. The Good Behavior Game has many applications and can be used to reduce disruption in such settings as assemblies, lunch periods, sports, and field trips.

A clever example of a good behavior game was described by Fishbein and Wasik (1981). It required the cooperation of the school counselor, the librarian, and the classroom teacher. One class was particularly disruptive in the library. The librarian seemed unable to manage these students and sought help from the school counselor. Together, they arranged for the implementation of the behavior game. The librarian held a session with those responsible in which they discussed and established a set of library rules of conduct. The students could earn points during library time that would earn them 10 minutes of working on a special art project or story in their regular classroom. This resulted in substantially improved behavior in the library.

The Timer Game is another version of the group contingency game for improved behavior. The Timer Game makes use of a simple kitchen timer

and was described by Broden, Hall, Dunlap, and Clark (1970). The object of the game is to earn points for studying. Each time the timer's bell rings (on the average every 8 minutes), any student who is studying earns one point. Each point earned allows the individual to leave for lunch 1 minute early. However, when a timer is used, the students should not be able to predict when it will ring. Sometimes the bell should ring almost immediately following a previous ring so the students do not expect a grace period for disruption.

Cooperative Learning Behavior Teams, suggested by Maurer (1988), divides students into teams consisting of three to four students. The group composition should be such that no group has more than one student who chronically displays disruptive behavior. A target behavior (i.e., a behavior to diminish or extinguish) should be chosen for all the groups to work on as they complete projects within groups. Team members remind each other about appropriate behavior. A group earns a point whenever any member of the group performs the target behavior. The goal for each team is to have accumulated the least number of points for demonstration of the target behavior by the end of the week. Thus, group members must help each other (e.g., by reminding, praising, reprimanding) to act appropriately and not earn a point. The group with the fewest points at the end of the week receives a reward.

TIPS FOR IMPLEMENTATION

1. Identify a target behavior that needs to be diminished yet is maintained because of group response.

2. Determine how the interdependent group contingency will be implemented.

3. Establish criterion level for attainment of a reward.

4. Have students identify the reward.

5. Identify the reward schedule (i.e., how often the reward will be given when criterion is reached).

6. Collect data to determine the success of the independent group contingency.

7. Be sure all students understand that, for the group to earn the reward, all students must be accountable for the target behavior.

8. Inform parents about the intervention so they are prepared to deal with comments about the plan's being "not fair." Some students will not have problems with the target behavior. They may report to their parents that they did not do the target behavior and that it is unfair that they cannot earn the reward until everyone behaves appropriately.

✔ **RESEARCH TO PRACTICE.** Gresham and Gresham (1982) compared the three versions of group contingencies (interdependent, dependent, and independent) and noted differential effects. The comparison, made during noninstructional classroom periods, pertained to the target behaviors of being out of seat, laughing inappropriately, verbal and physical aggression, and throwing objects. The interdependent and dependent contingencies were implemented as team games. In one, team members (half the class) won or lost the reward for each other; and in the other, the team captains earned the reward for their team. In the independent situation, each student competed against every other student. For these students, the interdependent situation produced the most successful results, and the independent situation was the least successful. The researchers made some interesting observations about the classroom occurrences during the three intervention conditions:

> Interdependent and dependent contingencies were more effective probably because of the element of group cooperation these contingencies introduced into the classroom. Students on each of the teams continually cued and praised respective team members or captains for emitting low rates of disruptive behavior. They also verbally reprimanded their peers whenever instances of disruptive behavior occurred. No such evidence of group cooperation was noted under the independent system. (p. 180)

Group contingencies are appealing for many reasons. They can add an element of fun and result in effective discipline and control without the heavy atmosphere that a rule-laden environment can produce. They can also be designed to influence small and large groups. They can be used to encourage improved performance in individual classrooms and schoolwide (e.g., one grade competing against the others). This intervention should result in overall improvement far greater than that resulting from targeting individuals' behaviors.

PRACTICE WHAT YOU'VE LEARNED

1. Identify instances of when dependent, independent, or interdependent group contingencies are appropriate. Cite specific classroom problems (e.g., tattling, talking out, fighting, arriving late to class) that could be remediated using one of these contingencies.

2. Design an intervention plan using one of the group contingencies, including data collection and evaluation procedures. Implement the plan and report on the results.

3. Provide examples of when each group contingency can be used in a preschool-, elementary-, or secondary-level setting. Discuss how the implementation procedures are the same and different across the three levels. Describe ways in which parents can be involved in this intervention.

4. Describe ways an interdependent group contingency can be implemented schoolwide. Identify specific schoolwide problems that can be reduced using this intervention. Describe ways in which the school faculty can work jointly on ensuring the success of this intervention.

SUMMARY

In this chapter,

1. Interventions found on the lower part of the Intervention Ladder were discussed.

2. These direct intervention procedures are simpler to use, less intrusive, and less severe than those found higher on the ladder.

3. This group of tactics should be considered before those discussed in Chapter 4.

4. These tactics are appropriate with a larger number of students and behavioral incidents.

As a review and summary, Table 3.3 presents a list of these interventions, along with the definition and an example of each.

CHAPTER DISCUSSION ACTIVITIES

1. Discuss some reasons for using interventions on the bottom portion of the ladder.

2. What are examples of mild and positive forms of direct intervention?

3. How and when are mild and positive forms of direct interventions implemented?

4. Describe the research that exists to support the efficacy of the interventions.

5. Explain examples of when to use the interventions.

BEHAVIORS AND INTERVENTIONS

1. Identify specific target behaviors from your own experience. Describe the intervention or pairing of interventions from this

TABLE 3.3
Glossary for the Intervention Ladder, Part I

Tactic	Definition	Example
SPECIFIC PRAISE	Providing students with positive statements and feedback about their appropriate conduct.	"Juan, thank you for waiting until everyone has finished their work to sharpen your pencils."
IGNORING	Systematically and consistently not paying attention to each occurrence of the target behavior.	When Susan came to the teacher's desk and interrupted Ms. Miller and Peter, who were working together on a special assignment, Ms. Miller and Peter paid no attention to her.
RULES	The entire class (teacher and pupils) determines a code of conduct for all to follow.	After several weeks of school, the class reviewed and finalized the guidelines about the behavior expected from each member. In addition to establishing a classroom code of conduct, they decided on some consequences for infractions of the rules.
CONTINGENT INSTRUCTIONS	After an occurrence of the target behavior, the teacher quietly and on a one-to-one basis tells the individual specifically not to engage in that activity.	While Steven was chewing gum in class, the teacher went to his desk and said to him quietly, "Don't chew gum at school, Steven."
CONTINGENT OBSERVATION	Removal of a disruptive student from a group activity, but still allowing the individual to observe the proceedings	During a group science activity, Bill was disruptive. His teacher had him return to his desk for 5 minutes while the others continued the science experiment.
CRITERION-SPECIFIC REWARDS	The student earns a special privilege only for reaching the desired level of the target behavior.	Because Tyler was not absent for a week of school, he was allowed 10 minutes of extra gym time on Friday afternoon.
FINES	The student loses privileges for engaging in the target behavior.	Emily became ineligible for this week's monitor duty because she was disruptive in the hall before school.

(continued)

TABLE 3.3
Continued

Tactic	Definition	Example
GROUP CONTINGENCIES		
Dependent	A person earns privileges or rewards for peers by behaving appropriately.	Susan earned the entire class 5 minutes of extra lunch time because she didn't argue with her teachers all morning.
Independent	Individuals earn reinforcement when they achieve a goal established for the group.	Each student who returned to campus on time after lunch break for 2 school weeks is excused from one academic period.
Interdependent	The class or group earns a special reward when the entire class meets the established goal.	When the entire class was not disruptive during history period Monday through Thursday, the weekly history test was cancelled.

chapter that will address the target behaviors. Share your information with others to gain additional ideas on how to deal effectively with the target behaviors.

2. Describe an intervention or pairing of interventions from this chapter that would address the following behaviors:

- Lateness to class
- Cussing
- Tipping in chair
- Talking out
- Sloppy work
- Fighting
- Cheating
- Forgetting materials
- Unfinished work

- Tattling
- No homework
- Out of seat
- Stealing
- Hall disruption
- Gum chewing
- Interrupting
- Argumentativeness
- Not listening

4

The Intervention Ladder, Part 2

OBJECTIVES

After reading this chapter, you should be able to

1. Explain reasons for using interventions from the upper part of the ladder.

2. Define difficult or more punitive forms of direct interventions.

3. Explain how and when to implement the interventions.

4. Cite research to support the efficacy of the interventions.

5. Provide examples of when to use the interventions.

6. Participate in "Practice What You've Learned" opportunities.

Interventions to be discussed in this chapter include

- **Peer Management**
Tutoring
Behavioral Managers
Environmental Restructuring
- **Self-Management**
Self-Regulation
Self-Evaluation
Self-Reinforcement
- **Parent Action**
- **Overcorrection**
Restitution
Positive Practice
- **Timeout**
Exclusion
Seclusion
- **Punishment**

• Exclusion
In-School Supervision
Suspension
Expulsion
• Involvement of Law Enforcement Agencies

Most of the interventions found higher on the Intervention Ladder have many positive elements and can produce beneficial effects for those students needing intervention to help them conform to the behavioral expectations of school environments and of their classmates. The direct intervention procedures found higher on the ladder, however, are more difficult to implement, or more intrusive to the learning environment, or more punitive. They require more teacher time initially. They usually require a change in the traditional instructional format, and sometimes are more negative, which could alter the positive educational climate. For these reasons, they should be implemented only when those procedures described in Chapter 3 have not produced the desired results.

DISCUSSION QUESTIONS

1. What interventions are located on the upper part of the Intervention Ladder?

2. Why are the interventions on the upper part of the Intervention Ladder more difficult to implement?

3. Which interventions might be viewed as punitive? Why is this so?

4. Why is more teacher time necessary to implement these interventions?

5. What types of changes in instructional format are necessary to implement these interventions?

6. Under what circumstances might teachers choose initially to implement interventions on the upper part of the ladder when disciplining students?

7. Which interventions might be more appropriate for pre-school-, elementary-, and secondary-level students?

PEER MANAGEMENT

The concept of students teaching students is not new. In fact, it was an integral part of the instructional process for the ancient Greeks and Romans and is relied on heavily in many European countries today. Three types of *peer management* are discussed: *peer tutoring*, *behavioral managers*, and *environmental restructuring*.

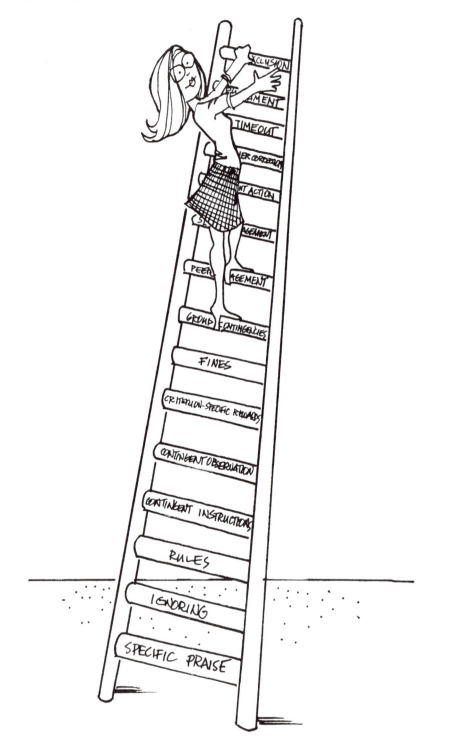

Peer Tutoring

DEFINITION

Peer tutoring means that one student proficient in an academic assignment serves in the role of teacher for a classmate who needs additional assistance.

Peer tutoring is the arrangement whereby students assist each other to learn academic subjects. Substantial research literature supports this practice (e.g., Devin-Sheehan, Feldman, & Allen, 1976; Jenkins & Jenkins, 1981; Maheady & Harper, 1987; Smith, 1989), particularly after the second grade. Clearly, more teachers should consider the adoption of a peer tutoring system, for it enhances the academic performance of all parties involved in the tutoring. Educators need to remember the positive relationship between academic achievement and disruption: As achievement increases, disruption declines. The implementation of peer tutoring to improve academic performance can positively influence social behavior as well. Students are a valuable resource when used effectively in the instructional process. Unfortunately, this resource is often left untapped.

DISCUSSION QUESTIONS

1. How can peer tutors be used in academic situations?
2. What training do peer tutors require to be successful?
3. What might be some limitations of peer tutors?
4. What are some advantages of peer tutors?

✔ **RESEARCH TO PRACTICE.** Peer tutors are helpful in various situations. First, peer tutors can help other students who require further directions or explanations, allowing teachers to conduct uninterrupted small-group instruction. Second, peer tutors can work with students who have received instruction in skills and require additional practice opportunities to master skills. Evertson, Emmer, Clements, Sanford, and Worsham (1984) identified several opportunities for students to serve as peer tutors: (a) working in pairs to complete academic tasks, (b) monitoring other students when the teacher is involved with small-group instruction, (c) serving as group leaders at learning stations, and (d) working as helpers for students who require assistance.

TIPS FOR IMPLEMENTATION

1. Be sure peer tutors are proficient in the skill they are tutoring.

2. Teach peer tutors how to provide specific praise.

3. Provide specific rules for peer tutoring situations, such as "Work quietly."

4. Be certain the peer tutor–tutee match is appropriate.

5. Provide places in the classroom for tutors to work quietly with other students.

6. Arrange for a cue so students can signal to tutors when assistance is needed.

7. Monitor peer tutoring to ensure that overreliance on the peer tutor is not occurring.

8. Teach tutors a variety of ways to practice skills.

Behavioral Managers

DEFINITION

A *behavioral manager* is a student whose classroom behavior is usually appropriate and earns the person the privilege of becoming the dispenser of praise and rewards for a peer.

In addition to helping in academic situations, peers can tutor each other on nonacademic tasks (Mercer, 1991). Tutors, in these situations, are usually referred to as behavioral managers. In this arrangement, well-behaved students assist others in improving their social behavior within the school setting. Behavioral managers are individuals who tutor fellow students to encourage reduced disruption and increased amounts of on-task behavior.

Guidelines for Tutoring Situations

Regardless of the tutoring assignment a student is given (academic tutor or behavioral manager), some important factors relate directly to the success of each tutoring situation.

SELECT THE TUTORS CAREFULLY.   First, the selection of the individual who will serve as tutor is critical. That person must want to serve in a tutorial role. Anyone who is forced to work with another student most likely will not possess the necessary motivation to fulfill the role successfully.

Second, the tutor needs to be knowledgeable of the subject matter to be taught. In academic situations, those who are not proficient in basic computational skills, for example, should not be selected as mathematics tutors. In behavioral instances, the pool of potential behavioral managers should comprise only those who demonstrate appropriate in-school behavior.

Third, because a one-to-one tutorial relationship is best, there must be a good fit between those who are to work together. Thus, the pairing of students is important. Chiang, Thorpe, and Darch (1980) pointed out the importance of compatibility between the two who are paired. Although they need not be best of friends, they should have a basic respect for each other and the role each is to play. The one selected as the behavioral manager should not be power hungry, but rather enter into the relationship in a spirit of cooperation and support. Students who have no regard for each other should not be paired, particularly when the target individual does not admire the behavioral manager in some way. The selection of the behavioral manager or academic tutor is therefore vital to the success of the program.

TRAIN THE TUTORS.   After a behavioral manager is selected, the tutor must be trained. The teacher or counselor needs to instruct the behavioral manager in the systematic use of behavioral techniques (described throughout this book). This student must know how to demonstrate the desired behavior and how to cue the tutored student to watch and then imitate proper, expected classroom deportment. In addition, the behavioral manager needs to learn how to give specific praise and deliver rewards for improved performance. Such training can usually be completed in several 15-minute sessions involving the potential behavioral manager and the adult who is supervising the project.

✔ RESEARCH TO PRACTICE.   Through the use of instruction and role playing, student tutors soon become proficient in the use of these simple behavioral techniques. In one such project reported by Strain (1981), for example, the peer trainers were (a) told the purpose of the intervention, (b) given

specific instructions about their training role, (c) allowed to role play the social limitations they were to use with their target pupils, and (d) reinforced for their role-playing attempts.

The success of the arrangement also rests on the behavioral manager's knowing exactly what is expected. In one highly successful tutorial project using eighth and ninth graders, Haisley, Tell, and Andrews (1981) found that a signed contract that clearly delineates the roles of each student facilitates the working relationship between both parties. Several factors are important:

1. The counselor or teacher must delineate clearly the parameters of the role. The behavioral manager must know what the limits are to the job.

2. The student needs to know what to do if the tutored pupil's deportment worsens or exceeds the limits of the behavioral manager's control.

3. Adult supervision and guidance are necessary, not only in the early stages of the arrangement, but throughout the process.

4. The students must not be left on their own, particularly when misconduct is the targeted area.

PROVIDE INCENTIVES AND REWARDS FOR TUTORS. One last point also affects the success of a tutorial relationship. In situations where tutoring is successful, tutors receive rewards for their efforts. At first, students feel honored by their selection. They seem very motivated to assist another individual in improving behavior, and are excited about becoming a "teacher." But experience and research indicate that the glory of being either a tutor or a behavioral manager is not lasting. For these students to remain interested and motivated to work toward the improvement of another student's performance, incentives for their effort are necessary. The person whose performance is improved receives rewards; so, too, should the one who facilitates and encourages that improvement. Usually, recognition for the tutor's accomplishments is sufficient reward, but this aspect of the tutorial relationship must not be ignored.

Benefits

Many studies that report the success of peer tutoring cite positive changes in the performances of both individuals, suggesting that this arrangement can benefit all involved. In academic situations, the achievement of both students (tutor and tutee) is enhanced. The same appears to be true in behavioral cases. Several authors, such as Chiang et al. (1980), have even indicated through their anecdotes that academic tutoring results in improved classroom deportment:

> The design of this study did not address the students' attitudinal changes. However, informal observations and teacher reports suggested

that the experience was of value to both tutors and tutees in terms of their general classroom behavior and attitude toward reading. (p. 18)

✔ **RESEARCH TO PRACTICE.** Researchers have studied a wide range of behaviors and complicated reinforcement systems in which behavioral managers have been used. Peers have managed very complicated reinforcement procedures and very simple ones. They have modified behaviors such as aggression, general disruption, studying, independent working, and compliance. Clearly, peers can be used to facilitate the improved social behavior patterns of their classmates. In one study (Lovitt, Lovitt, Eaton, & Kirkwood, 1973), a student with learning disabilities served as a behavioral manager for a peer with learning problems.

> Ivan and Curtis, both 9 years old, were classmates. Curtis served as Ivan's behavioral manager. Ivan often disrupted the class by making inappropriate verbalizations that might best be referred to as "bathroom language." These comments particularly bothered Curtis, who said to Ivan, after each outrageous verbalization, "I don't like to sit by you when you say . . . ." He then picked up his schoolwork and moved to another desk. Soon, the frequency of the distracting verbalizations fell to zero.

This example demonstrates that, if the dynamics of the situation are right, the qualifications necessary to become a behavioral manager need not be overwhelming. It also shows that a teacher does not have to intervene directly to modify disruption. One boy's systematic use of a reprimand and his withdrawal from the presence of the offensive student produced the desired results: a more positive environment for the entire class. One nice aspect of peer management is that the teacher does not have to spend valuable instructional time attending to disruption. Because peers often inadvertently participate in and encourage their peers' disruption, as discussed previously, it is appropriate to involve them in its reduction.

Environmental Restructuring

DEFINITION

In *environmental restructuring*, the class is instructed and reinforced for encouraging a classmate's appropriate behavior.

Another positive way to involve peers in the improved performance of a classmate is environmental restructuring, which has its origins in the brilliant work with disturbed youth by two psychologists, Nicholas Hobbs and William Rhodes. Their basic premise was that modifying the behavior of a target student is not sufficient for overall and long-lasting treatment; rather, the environment in which these students find themselves in trouble must also be changed. In other words, behavior does not exist in isolation; the interplay between the individual and the physical and social environment in which he or she is placed largely explains why certain behaviors are exhibited and maintained. As discussed in the section in Chapter 3 on group contingencies, classmates can encourage, either directly or indirectly, inappropriate conduct. For example, the "class clown" jokes around only because his classmates attend to him, laugh at his antics or jokes, and thereby reinforce undesirable behavior. The teacher can arrange various interventions to discourage the target students from disrupting the class, but once the teacher's direct intervention discontinues, chances are that the inappropriate behaviors will reoccur as the student attempts to regain the attention of his peers. In such cases where long-term effects of interventions are not achieved, environmental restructuring is one positive alternative that should be considered.

Stages in Environmental Restructuring

The process of environmental restructuring involves three stages: (a) group discussion; (b) instruction in the use of systematic praise, modeling, contingent instructions, ignoring, and role playing; and (c) rewards.

STAGE 1.   In the initial stages of environmental restructuring, the classmates of the student(s) who engage in disruption should have several discussion sessions guided by the counselor or teacher. The purpose of these meetings is to have students (a) pinpoint the behaviors that disturb the learning environment, (b) realize their role in encouraging and maintaining those behaviors, and (c) develop a helping attitude and concern about the individuals who are disruptive and the behaviors they display. In this regard, it is important to point out to the group that almost everyone at some time has engaged in the targeted undesirable behaviors, but that it is the frequency and intensity of these acts that result in the disruption of the learning climate. The class also needs to recognize their active and passive participation in this undesirable situation. These students must come to a realization that they, too, are at fault and can actively seek to change their behavior (and, thereby, the behavior of their disruptive classmates). Once this level of understanding is achieved, instruction in the use of the various intervention strategies can be initiated.

STAGE 2.   At this point, the counselor or teacher needs to teach the class how to systematically *praise* the target student for appropriate classroom conduct. The students should be instructed in ways to *model* proper behavior and to unobtrusively cue their targeted classmate to watch them respond in appropriate fashions. It is helpful for the class to learn how to use *contingent instructions* effectively and how to quietly and privately reprimand when behavioral infractions occur. In addition, they must learn to *ignore* behavior designed to attract their attention. This task is most important, yet is very difficult for many. It is difficult to not laugh or smile at a joke or funny act. This requires much practice, and *role playing* can be helpful in this regard. Gamelike situations can be arranged in which fellow students try to get the attention of the class by their actions and the class attempts to ignore these contrived antics.

STAGE 3.   In the final stage, the students should be rewarded for their efforts. As indicated previously, environmental restructuring requires cooperation from the entire group. The expectations of the group are high and often difficult to execute. Members of the group should, of course, be recognized for their efforts. Students who generally follow school codes of conduct are seldom motivated to restructure their environment merely to establish an atmosphere conducive to learning. Additional honors, recognition, privileges, or rewards should be offered to the *entire* class (including the target student) for their efforts. Although this process involves a considerable amount of the teacher's time to initiate and to supervise, once underway, the benefits to participants can be monumental: The target student's conduct undergoes long-lasting changes, and the others learn about the interrelationships between their active and passive actions and the behavior of another.

PRACTICE WHAT YOU'VE LEARNED

1. Design a peer tutoring plan that targets students who should be working independently at their seats yet require teacher assistance during small-group instruction.

2. List behaviors for which behavioral manager intervention would be appropriate.

3. Develop an environmental restructuring plan to assist a secondary-level student who likes to tell jokes to his neighbors during class instruction. Use the stages discussed above in your plan.

4. Describe ways a cross-age/grade level peer tutoring program could be established at the elementary and secondary level.

5. Identify a target behavior in your classroom for which peer tutoring, behavioral managing, or environmental restructuring would be appropriate. Describe an intervention plan. Include a method of data collection to ensure the plan is working.

SELF-MANAGEMENT

Over the last decade, a growing interest by both researchers and educators has centered on the use of self-management procedures to improve school performance. Researchers have shown that self-management techniques are efficacious for both elementary (e.g., Hughes & Boyle, 1991) and secondary (e.g., Schloss, 1987) students. Besides having been proven effective in enhancing both academic and social skills of students, these procedures are appealing because they require the individual to become actively involved in the school program. Many students, although very active in the ways they behave in school, are only passively involved in their own school programs. Ellis and Friend (1991) and Ellis (1986) pointed out that adolescent students with learning disabilities tend to rely on their teachers to achieve success in the classroom rather than taking a more active and responsible role in the instructional process. Such an overreliance is counterproductive to promoting independence in individuals who will soon become adults and must be capable of self-responsibility and decision making. Some have an "I don't care" attitude, and do not see the importance of making an effort to contribute to their learning environment. One possible reason for this is their lack of involvement in the school curriculum and related activities. The use of self-management procedures seems to change these students' dispositions, thereby making them active learners seeking to modify their own behavior patterns.

In addition to yielding positive short-term results, self-management tactics encourage students to learn valuable life skills. In most school situations, the student has few choices: The curriculum is set by school administrators, the instructional materials and assignments are chosen by teachers, and the rules of conduct in many cases are established by others. The school experience often consists only of an externally structured set of tasks, obligations, and expectations. Fagen, Long, and Stevens (1975) reported that this lack of "freedom of choice" in our schools has far-reaching and negative implications. They pointed out that individuals, after graduation from school, must join society as productive citizens who make an incredible number of choices each day. Adults must possess the personal skills necessary to control their behavior in a variety of ways. For example, they must have the self-control to work successfully with others in job situations, to manage spending according to their financial limitations, and to schedule leisure time appropriately. Although the freedom of adulthood seems unlimited to students, it is not.

Students need to be prepared for the challenge of making choices for themselves. Despite the realities facing students after graduation, educators tend not to prepare them for the eventual requirements of adult life. The battery of tactics referred to as self-management procedures can contribute positively to learning about self-control, self-scheduling, self-evaluation, and self-reinforcement.

DISCUSSION QUESTIONS

1. Why are self-management interventions important to use?

2. Why are self-management interventions located on the upper part of the ladder?

3. What are examples of practices that promote student dependence on teachers?

4. What are ways to turn dependence into independence in the examples listed in Question 3?

5. How can general education and special education teachers work together to use self-management interventions?

6. What self-management interventions are appropriate for young children?

7. What self-management interventions can be started at the elementary level to prepare students better for secondary-level teacher expectations?

Many excellent and comprehensive reviews have been written on the use of self-management (Lovitt, 1984; Rosenbaum & Drabman, 1979; Workman, 1982). In the following sections, three specific kinds of self-management strategies are discussed: *self-regulation*, which encourages individuals to regulate their own behavior and learn how to control themselves in difficult situations; *self-evaluation*, which involves students in evaluating their behavior and its improvement; and *self-reinforcement*, which has the students reinforce or reward themselves when improvement is noted.

Self-Regulation

DEFINITION

In *self-regulation*, individuals monitor their own behavior, seek to avoid those situations that precipitate inappropriate behavior, and stop that behavior if it is initiated.

The aim of most self-regulation procedures is to reduce the frequency of undesirable behavior patterns by teaching behavioral self-control. The assumption is that most students can learn how to control their behavior (Lovitt, 1984). Self-regulation has been used for a wide range of incidents, ranging from the mild to the very serious. For example, a tactic referred to as the *turtle technique* (O'Leary & O'Leary, 1977; Robin, Schneider, & Dolnick, 1977) was used successfully to reduce aggression. With this technique, the student is taught to delay reacting to a situation by closing her eyes, clenching her fists, and resting her head on the desk. While the student relaxes, she is to think of alternate ways to handle the situation. This procedure helps students to calm themselves when troubled or frustrated, thereby helping them to control their temper and avoid disruptive outbursts. The technique leads to additional benefits, for the class is not disrupted and the target student can usually return to productive school work more quickly.

Self-regulation techniques can be taught to students by counselors and classroom teachers. Explanations of how this can be done are provided below.

SELF-REGULATION TECHNIQUES TAUGHT BY COUNSELORS.   Counselors who wish to implement an entire curriculum that teaches self-control to those who have serious inabilities to control themselves should refer to Fagen et al. (1975) and Fagen and Long (1976). These authors described techniques to teach students how to anticipate situations, appreciate feelings, manage frustration, inhibit or delay their negative reactions, and relax. The following example illustrates these techniques.

Richard occasionally fought on the playground. After these instances, he usually verbalized his sorrow and indicated that he did not really want to fight but had to defend a friend or preserve his pride. The counselor, through a series of observations and discussions with Richard, helped the student identify those events that typically preceded the fights. They mutually determined that there were plenty of warnings to indicate when a fight was imminent, and that a series of events (verbal statements, the arrangement of certain students) usually preceded an actual fight. After Richard was able to identify these, the counselor discussed with Richard what options he had at each warning.

For example, Richard could avoid playing games with certain students, and when verbal abuses were initiated by others, he could walk away. At all points, Richard was encouraged to talk through the situations and the options he had. The counselor helped the student to practice selecting behavioral options by role playing various incidents. Soon Richard learned how to avoid situations that led to fights, and his frequency of fighting decreased to zero.

DISCUSSION QUESTIONS

1. What situations must Richard identify?

2. What feelings must Richard anticipate?

3. What are effective ways Richard can manage his frustration and feelings?

4. What are some ways the counselor can teach Richard self-regulation?

If this overall approach is adopted, then (a) special sessions should be arranged for those who need such specific instruction; (b) this group should meet several times a week for instruction; and (c) to ensure carry-over to the regular class, teachers who are assigned these students should receive information and supervision from the counselor to further the goals of the program.

SELF-REGULATION TECHNIQUES TAUGHT BY TEACHERS.   Self-regulation also is used by teachers to help individuals deal with more minor situations. Through discussion sessions and practice, teachers are taught to judge situations before they respond. In the following example, a student learns how to implement the self-regulation intervention.

Fred often got into trouble in the corridor when going from third- to fourth-period class. He usually stopped at his locker between these periods to drop off books from earlier classes and to pick up his books and assignments for the rest of the day. Several students were usually at the adjacent lockers while Fred was at his locker. These students were rowdy and verbally abusive. They seemed to pick on students who were in the area at the same time. Fred's typical response was to return the verbally abusive language. At times, Fred was misidentified as the troublemaker by a passing teacher who attempted to stop the behavior. Fred would arrive at his fourth-period class late and upset.

Fred's teacher monitored his behavior for a week, noting the number of days he entered the classroom upset. The teacher spoke with Fred about what was occurring between classes. Together they identified the problem behavior and when it would occur. The teacher helped Fred determine an effective self-regulation plan for dealing with the situation. The teacher asked Fred questions, such as, What seems to be the problem? When does it occur? Who is around? What are you doing about it now? How does that strategy work? and What might be other more effective ways of dealing with the problem? Fred's plan was to go to his locker at a different time during the day when the boys were not around. He also decided that if the boys arrived, he would close his locker immediately and walk away. Fred and the teacher decided to meet weekly to assess the effectiveness of Fred's plan. Meanwhile, the teacher monitored Fred's behavior when he arrived at class to see if he appeared calm and in control.

This example demonstrates one technique, the problem-solving process, used to help students learn to analyze their own behavior: (a) identify problems, (b) determine why they occur, (c) predict when an undesirable behavior has a high probability of happening, and (d) learn how to avoid these incidents. The benefits of this approach include that the undesired behaviors reduce in frequency, and the individual is left with a valuable skill that can be applied in other negative situations.

Specific Techniques.   A variety of specific self-regulation techniques are available for teachers to consider when teaching students how to control their behavior. Some of these techniques are (a) counting softly to calm down; (b) self-timing out in an area that allows the student quiet and seclusion until self-control is regained; (c) removing oneself from a problem situation, such as walking away or leaving the room; and (d) using self-talk to remind oneself to show behavioral control. The teacher's role is to (a) help students, through the problem-solving process, to develop a self-regulation plan; (b) reinforce students for implementing their plan; and (c) work with students to evaluate the effectiveness of the plan.

Selection of Techniques. The selection of a self-regulation technique is student specific. The teacher must keep in mind several factors:

1. The previously implemented self-regulation techniques should be evaluated to determine the reason for their success or failure. It is important to note what behaviors were paired with the techniques and why those techniques did or did not work effectively with the behaviors.

2. The setting in which the behavior occurs may affect the type of self-regulatory intervention chosen. For example, the turtle technique may be appropriate for a classroom setting, but may not work as well if the student is walking down the hallway when the problem behavior occurs.

3. The student's age and ability level are important. These factors may affect the type of intervention chosen and the amount of practice needed to teach the intervention.

4. The behavior of concern will influence the type of self-regulatory intervention chosen. For instance, if the student is self-regulating his or her talking-out behavior, the turtle technique probably is not the best choice.

Self-Evaluation

DEFINITION

In *self-evaluation*, students correct their own performance, record the frequency, and graph the resulting data.

In another version of self-management, sometimes referred to as self-evaluation, the student is required to monitor and evaluate his or her own performance. Researchers have found that self-evaluating procedures have a positive effect on student performance (Harris, 1986; Hughes & Boyle, 1991). Accordingly, self-evaluation procedures prove to be highly motivating for students, resulting in improvements with the target behavior (Lovitt, 1984). Several steps are involved in implementing this intervention: (a) recognizing whether a behavior is correct, (b) recording occurrences of the behavior, and (c) graphing the results and evaluating the behavior.

DESIGNING A SELF-EVALUATION INTERVENTION PLAN

Recognizing Behaviors. The first step in designing a self-evaluation plan is to teach students how to recognize occurrences and nonoccurrences of the target behavior. For instance, self-correcting an arithmetic worksheet is a rather simple example: The arithmetic problem is either correct or not. For a student who is having difficulty discriminating appropriate from inappropriate behavior, however, recognizing occurrences and nonoccurrences of a target behavior might prove to be a difficult but important task.

✔ **RESEARCH TO PRACTICE.** Some elementary teachers have helped students understand what is appropriate and what is not by taping illustrations of the desired and undesired behaviors on the students' desks (see Kunzelmann, Cohen, Hutten, Martin, & Mingo, 1970, and Lovitt, 1984, for a discussion about *countoons*). The picture cues denote what the appropriate and inappropriate behavior looks like and help students to identify more readily what they are expected to do. For example, a picture of a student with his or her mouth wide open might be used to depict talking out, whereas the opposite picture would show the student with his or her mouth shut and hand raised.

Hallahan, Lloyd, Kosiewicz, Kauffman, and Graves (1979) taught a student the difference between attending and nonattending in two steps. In the first step, the teacher modeled both attending and nonattending when completing school work. The teacher labeled each set of behaviors so the student knew exactly what (i.e., attending or nonattending) was being demonstrated. In the second step, the teacher role played different situations, and the student had to label each as an example of attending or nonattending behavior.

Recording Occurrences of Behaviors. The second step in designing the self-evaluation plan is to teach students to record instances of the desired and undesired behavior. The following vignette exemplifies how students can learn to record their own behavior.

> Sarah had a tendency to use profanity, complain, and argue during seatwork assignments. This distracted the teacher and others who were seated around Sarah. The teacher drew a small cartoon on an index card and taped it to Sarah's desk. On one side was a picture of a girl working quietly at her desk, and on the other was a picture of a girl not working appropriately. To help prompt Sarah, every 2 minutes the teacher asked her to place a mark under the drawing that illustrated her behavior at that moment. At the end of the period, the teacher and Sarah evaluated and discussed the number of times she was and was not working in the desired manner.

In this example, the self-evaluation included a self-recording feature: Sarah collected data on her own performance. She was instructed to place a mark under the drawing that best illustrated her behavior during a period of time. The teacher and student then evaluated the results. In some cases, teachers record instances of the desired and undesired behavior and compare their results with the students' results. This is a good periodic reliability check to be sure that students are aware of occurrences of the desired and undesired behaviors and that those results are recorded accurately.

✔ **RESEARCH TO PRACTICE.**   Hallahan et al. (1979) used a tape recording of a tone that sounded periodically. The student was instructed to record a check in the yes or no box depending on whether the student was attending to the task when the tone sounded. The researchers found through this and subsequent self-monitoring and self-evaluation studies that on-task behavior increased, academic productivity increased somewhat, maintenance effects were recorded for up to 2½ months, and the best results were obtained when the student recorded his or her own performance (Hallahan et al., 1983).

Excellent research data are available on self-recording (sometimes called self-monitoring). Data indicate that merely recording the number of times one engages in the desired behavior can result in dramatic improvement. For example, in one of the first studies of self-recording, Broden, Hall, and Mitts (1971) found that merely by keeping self-records of the amount of time spent studying and talking, students became less disruptive and more studious. Self-monitoring also has resulted in students increasing the amount of time they spend on a task (Hallahan, Marshall, & Lloyd, 1981; Kneedler & Hallahan, 1981; Lloyd, Hallahan, Kosiewicz, & Kneedler, 1982), the by-product of which is less disruption. Kneedler and Hallahan (1981) also indicated that students do not have to be accurate in their self-recording for desired results to be achieved.

Graphing and Evaluating the Results.   The third step in designing the self-evaluation plan requires the student to graph the recordings and evaluate the results. Some teachers have taught students to keep graphs of the daily data that they collect on their behavior. This seems to have great appeal for many students, particularly at the middle school level. In a project described by Lowe and Smith (1982), students were taught to evaluate their own performance by collecting data and placing it on a daily graph. This activity served as an excellent motivator, and students also learned the important skill of graphing.

Lloyd et al. (1982) offered some explanations for the effectiveness of self-recording:

The act of committing one's judgment about one's performance to a recording sheet requires careful evaluation of one's performance. Thus, the reactive effects of self-recording may be greater because subjects realize that when they make public record of their judgments, they are less able to deceive anyone about their performance. (p. 224)

Self-Reinforcement

DEFINITION

Self-reinforcement is the rewarding of oneself for correct behavior.

The last version of self-management discussed is self-reinforcement. When this procedure is used, students determine what their reinforcement is to be if they perform at a certain level.

✔ **RESEARCH TO PRACTICE.** In one of the first self-management research studies conducted, Lovitt and Curtiss (1969) demonstrated students' ability to select their own schedules of reinforcement. In that study, performance was far better when the teacher administered the reinforcement. During the 1970s, a number of studies were conducted that compared teacher-imposed and self-determined reinforcement. The results of those studies (Billingsley, 1977; Felixbrod & O'Leary, 1973; Glynn, 1970) indicated that both teacher-imposed and self-determined reinforcement achieve better results than no reinforcement, but that one is not significantly more effective than the other. These findings countered the earlier results of Lovitt and Curtiss. In another well-controlled study (Dickerson & Creedon, 1981), self-reinforcement clearly produced better results than teacher-imposed reinforcement. Thus, the benefits of self-reinforcement appear to be multifold: (a) they produce substantial desired improvement in performance, (b) they actively involve students in their learning environment, and (c) they serve to teach a skill beneficial to independent adult living.

Some information about self-reinforcement has emerged that is surprising to most educators, who presume that, when students are allowed to determine their own rewards, they set standards for themselves that are easy to attain and yield great amounts of reinforcement. However, Dickerson and Creedon (1981) found that the subjects of their research established stringent standards (possibly because the teachers stayed in the room while standards were set, and once they were set they could not be changed). They also observed an interesting by-product of self-reinforcement. While this condition was in effect, students requested their classmates to be less dis-

ruptive with statements such as, "Can't you be quiet? We're supposed to be working" and "Leave me alone. I want to work" (pp. 431–432). The researchers also observed several of the students praising themselves for improved school performance.

In another study, Fantuzzo and Clement (1981) noted other interesting consequences of self-reinforcement. In one condition one student in the class was given reinforcement by the teacher, and in another condition that same student was allowed to reward himself for being on task. In both instances, earned points were redeemable for treats. In the final condition of the study, the rest of the class members were allowed to monitor their own behavior but did not receive the contingent rewards. When the teacher rewarded the target student, the other students' behavior did not change.

However, when the target student rewarded himself, the other students' on-task behavior also improved. When students were given the opportunity to self-monitor how well they paid attention to the teacher, their on-task behavior again improved. It appears, then, that self-reinforcement is superior to teacher-imposed rewards. Moreover, teachers can expect the performance of the entire class to improve even though they are not being rewarded, a beneficial by-product of intervention.

Thomas (1980) noted another benefit of using self-management procedures. He found not only that they are both efficient and effective, but that they result in better maintenance and generalization of treatment effects because they exist without external environmental supports. He claimed that, once these procedures are in effect, the teacher will have more time to devote to instruction.

TIPS FOR IMPLEMENTATION

1. Identify behaviors for which self-reinforcement is an appropriate intervention.

2. Identify potential reinforcers through discussion with students.

3. Have students discuss what level of behavior must occur for a certain amount of reinforcement.

4. Have students provide their own reinforcement when earned.

Self-Regulation, Self-Evaluation, Self-Reinforcement

Nelson and Hayes (1981) stressed that all three types of self-management (self-regulation, self-evaluation, and self-reinforcement) should be employed concurrently. They maintained that, throughout the process, students must observe, monitor, and reward their own behavior. This serves as a cue or trigger for self-adjustive behaviors. During the self-reinforcement stage, the individual verifies his or her behavior against a standard and has the motivation to continue improvement toward that standard. These authors summarized the process as follows: "First, . . . the reactive chain begins by self-monitoring (either noticing one's own behavior and/or recording its occurrence); and, second, that self-monitored behavior increases or decreases in frequency as a function of self-administered consequences" (p. 5). These observations help to explain why self-management produces superior results.

PRACTICE WHAT YOU'VE LEARNED

1. Specify classroom behaviors for which self-regulation, self-evaluation, and self-reinforcement would be appropriate interventions.

2. Identify a student for whom one of the self-management (or a combination of the three) interventions would be useful. Design the intervention plan, including a method to monitor student progress.

3. Identify a student who would benefit from the self-regulation intervention. Describe how the intervention would be taught to the student. Describe ways to actively involve the student in the design of the intervention plan.

4. Discuss ways the self-management techniques could be used on a schoolwide basis.

5. Describe the role of the teacher at the elementary and secondary level when designing, implementing, and evaluating a self-management intervention plan.

PARENT ACTION

DEFINITION

Parent action involves the parents in designing an intervention plan that can be implemented both at school and at home.

The importance of involving parents in their child's education throughout the school year was emphasized in Chapter 2. Communication between home and school should be a continual process, for education should be a team effort involving all those who are concerned for the well-being and educational progress of each student. A common practice in the past, and unfortunately in many cases today, is that educators approach parents only when students are experiencing problems at school. This situation places parents and teachers in an adversarial position that is neither productive nor fruitful, for it does not result in a positive working relationship between educators and parents. Clearly, many minor difficulties at school could be minimized or avoided if parents were actively involved in their students' total school lives. As discussed earlier, some educators discourage ongoing parent involvement, so they find it difficult to call upon parents to assist in an intervention program aimed at improving school deportment.

One reason why parent action for intervention is placed high on the Intervention Ladder centers on the notion that parents should be contacted more often about positive gains their children make at school. If teachers

and counselors resort to parent involvement for each minor infraction (which should be eliminated or reduced through the procedures previously discussed), the frequency of parent contacts would be high but mainly negative in content. To reduce the probability of this situation, we suggest that parent action in designing an intervention be tried only after tactics lower on the Intervention Ladder have proven unsuccessful. Furthermore, before tactics appearing higher on the ladder are employed, parents should be informed, and in some cases their permission should be obtained. By involving parents at this point and showing them the evaluation results (see Chapter 5) of previous unsuccessful interventions, parents become aware of school difficulties. If more serious interventions become necessary, parents have been given the opportunity to assist in remediation efforts. Too often, parents are unaware of problems at school until drastic measures are in force. Parents' surprise and shock of learning that their children are not "model students" can place school personnel in a difficult and negative position.

TIPS FOR IMPLEMENTATION

1. Develop and implement a parent contact system at the beginning of the school year. This could involve a weekly note home or phone call to provide progress information. The focus should be on positive gains and behavior, but mention should be made of those areas that need to be stressed further.

2. Establish a parent involvement program in which parents can choose ways to become involved in the classroom.

3. Inform parents that conferences can be arranged at different times during the day to accommodate varying parental schedules.

4. Keep parents informed.

Guidelines for Initiating Parent Action

If interventions on the lower part of the ladder are unsuccessful, it may be necessary to invite parents to school to establish an intervention plan that can be carried out mutually between home and school. This type of parental action is often acceptable to parents if good rapport has been established with the teacher and a sense of trust and respect has evolved over the course of the school year. When parents are asked to assist in an intervention plan, several steps are followed: (a) conducting the conference, (b) designing the intervention plan, and (c) monitoring the implementation of the intervention.

CONDUCTING THE CONFERENCE.   Several parent conferences may be held when parent action is necessary to initiate an intervention plan. Educators must be prepared for the conferences and aware of certain behaviors that promote a positive partnership with the parents.

Preconference Activities.   Before the initial conference, the school personnel who will attend should be identified. The best situation is to involve the counselor and all of the educators who are having difficulty with the target student. Prior to a parent meeting, the staff involved should become familiar with the student's record. Data about the kind of conduct problems and the frequency of their occurrence should be gathered. Anecdotal records should document when serious disruptions have occurred and a description of the nature of the disruptions. In addition, the educators involved should indicate what other intervention procedures have been tried and what results were achieved.

Initial Conference Activities.   The initial parent conference is very important to the ultimate success of a cooperative effort aimed at improving the school performance of any student. The factors that must be considered for an effective parent conference include (a) establishing a convenient time to meet, (b) focusing on approaches and interactions that will promote a good working relationship, and (c) learning about the parent's ability to initiate an intervention plan.
    • Time. The time a parent conference is scheduled is important. In today's society, many students have parents who both work outside the home and have difficulty leaving work for a parent conference. If parents perceive that their attendance is required at an inconvenient time, they can be resentful, and may not give their full attention to the meeting. Therefore, the conference time should be arranged for the mutual convenience of all parties involved. This may necessitate an early morning or late afternoon meeting. In other cases, an evening conference may be necessary to ensure parent participation.
    • Approaches. The manner in which educators approach parents is critical. Many parents comment that their contacts with school personnel are unpleasant. One reason for this is that the only time they are called to school is when the topic is negative, but another reason is the way educators interact with parents. Some educators view parents as hostile and ignorant

about schools, even though many parents are professionals who are successful in their own careers. These adults are not accustomed to being treated like students or inferiors and resent the way some school personnel treat them. If a cooperative and productive relationship is to develop, the parents' individual needs and abilities should be determined. Above all, parents must be treated with respect.

Mercer (1991) identified specific steps teachers should take to ensure a positive conference. He stated that teachers should identify the purpose for meeting, ask open-ended questions, clarify and reflect as necessary, and avoid discussing topics not relevant to the purpose. Some ideas for approaching parents in a positive mode include (a) ensuring that furniture is comfortable and appropriate for adults; (b) avoiding talking down to parents; (c) avoiding unnecessary educational jargon that may create misunderstandings; (d) limiting the number of professionals at the initial conference, if possible, to minimize feelings of intimidation; (e) asking parents what goals are important for them to see their child attain; (f) telling parents that notes will be taken and reviewed so that important points are recorded accurately; (g) providing parents with copies of notes for their future reference; (h) making sure that positive behaviors are noted about the student; (i) sharing data about the behavior of concern and results of previous interventions; (j) emphasizing the importance of working together to help the student progress; and (k) ending the conference on a positive note.

• Parental Abilities. In addition to sharing information about the student during the initial parent conference, educators must gain the necessary information about the parents to determine the role that these specific parents can assume. Some parents are able to follow through with intervention programs designed by school personnel, whereas others can help design as well as implement these programs. Some parents require counseling themselves. Other parents are unable to participate positively in school–home intervention programs. Many school districts and community agencies now offer parent training or parent counseling sessions, and the school counselor or teacher might want to refer some parents to such groups. For those counselors who wish to establish their own parent training groups, excellent manuals, articles, and materials are available (Buckley & Walker, 1978; Cooper & Edge, 1978; Hallenback & Beernick, 1989; Kramer, 1990; Wagonseller & McDowell, 1982; Wolf & Stephens, 1990).

During this important initial session, a climate of trust and cooperation between home and school must be established. The educators need to assess the parent's abilities to work positively to improve the student's behavior and share data about the student's school deportment.

Designing the Intervention Plan

If educators determine that a parent or set of parents can participate in an intervention program, then another conference session should be scheduled. The type and complexity of intervention programs facilitated or implemented by parents need to be individually tailored to the parents' abilities, interests, and time constraints. The amount of time they can contribute to the program, their willingness to participate in a positive way, and their consistency in application all need to be considered when the plan is designed. Considerable evidence indicates that parents can be effective agents of change in their students' lives, both at home and at school. They have modified extreme as well as minor problems. In the following sections, some suggestions are offered about intervention schemes that have proven successful with parents and educators serving as partners.

PARENTS ADMINISTERING REWARDS.   A great variety of items and events can serve as reinforcers that parents can deliver at home. Just as at school, privileges can be offered for improved school performance. Teachers and counselors might assist parents in determining appropriate rewards. However, as discussed earlier, caution must be taken because adults are not reliable selectors of motivators for students. According to parents, the following are some rewards that students like to receive: extra allowances, being read to by a parent, a movie on Saturday, attendance at a sporting event, a special dinner, or extra television time.

The following are several important considerations for parents who are arranging a reinforcement system at home:

1. They must be able to deliver the reward. A reward promised but not delivered can result in worsened performance.

2. They must be consistent in its application. If the reward is not earned, it must not be given. If the family is planning a special event on Saturday and the student must go regardless of his or her performance, that event should not be offered as a reward.

3. Through training and consultation, educators can help parents determine the reasonableness of the rewards offered. Rewards should match the behavior criteria. Providing large or expensive rewards sets up students for expecting a great reward for demonstrating appropriate behavior.

4. Parents also can fine their children for inappropriate behavior; however, they must refrain from being too harsh. If fines are

used, school personnel should assist parents in determining the severity of the fines.

Throughout all phases of a school–home intervention plan, educators must supervise the program and continue communication with parents about progress at school. Once parents are included in school affairs, they need to remain included. Although parent action can require increased time from educators, the benefits in most cases are well worth the time and effort.

✔ **RESEARCH TO PRACTICE.** In a number of studies, parents have served as the administrators of a reward system. In one of the first studies of this kind (McKenzie, Clark, Wolf, Kothera, & Benson, 1968), when students received weekly grades from their teachers and when their parents determined weekly allowances on the basis of the grades received, the students' grades increased dramatically.

Ayllon, Garber, and Pisor (1975) achieved a dramatic reduction in classroom disruption through a system in which the teachers used daily good behavior letters. If a student went home with a good behavior letter, he or she had met the criterion for acceptable classroom behavior, and the parent delivered a reward. Through this system, classroom disruption, initially at 90%, fell to an acceptable level of 10%. The use of notes or daily behavior report cards has proven to be very popular with parents and educators, and has been used successfully with kindergartners, elementary pupils, and middle school and high school students. In most cases, it results in positive improvements at school and serves to increase communication between school and home. It is an easy-to-manage system that promotes an excellent partnership and continuity between these two very important aspects of students' lives.

Monitoring the Implementation of the Intervention

Communication and dialogue must continue after the initial conference, and a method for that continued communication must be determined. For example, informal notes or periodic phone calls between school and home can facilitate communication. Rutherford and Edgar (1979) offered some valuable suggestions about such contacts. They suggested that a favorable ratio of positive to negative comments be used and monitored: For every negative comment in a phone conversation or note sent home, four positive items of information should be included. Such a ratio will encourage better relationships with parents and will keep the communication lines open. Kroth and Simpson (1977) added that data should be kept on parent contacts and, for some parents, an anecdotal record regarding the nature and content of each contact. (A sample record-keeping form is shown in Figure 4.1.) If the decision is made that specific parents are unable to help with the intervention plan, then school personnel should contact these parents to keep them informed about progress at school.

PRACTICE WHAT YOU'VE LEARNED

1. Identify types of data to obtain prior to an initial conference with parents.

2. Discuss how parent conferences are similar and different at the elementary and secondary levels.

3. Describe ways to establish rapport with parents at the beginning of the school year.

4. List ways to help parents feel at ease in a conference.

5. Discuss different types of parent reactions that might be encountered in a conference designed to obtain cooperation for a home-based intervention plan. Indicate ways to deal with different types of parent reaction.

6. Identify ways to maintain ongoing home–school communication and monitoring of the intervention plan.

7. Generate a list of possible home-administered rewards.

OVERCORRECTION

Overcorrection requires individuals to assume responsibility for their actions (Axelrod, Brantner, & Meddock, 1978). There are two forms of overcorrection: *restitutional overcorrection* and *positive practice overcorrection*. Unlike the tactics listed higher on the Intervention Ladder, overcorrection procedures are considered to have an educational component. Despite the negative or punitive aspects of overcorrection, they have gained in popularity and use in schools (e.g., Carey & Bucher, 1983; Foxx & Bechtel, 1983).

Student's Name: *Megan*

Parent's Name: *Valerie & Tom Finn*

Teacher's Name: *Francine Bell*

Academic Year: *1992-1993*

Date	Type of Contact	Who Contacted	By Whom	Content
9/6	phone call	Valerie Finn	Bell	reminder about parent conference
9/8	formal parent-teacher conference	both parents	Bell	overall progress and progress in writing; talked about awareness problem
9/22	note sent home	both parents	Bell	good behavior report
9/27	note sent home	both parents	Bell	good behavior report; evening incident on playground
10/2	chat after school	Valerie Finn	Bell	discussed evening incident

FIGURE 4.1. Sample record-keeping form for frequency and type of parent contact.

Restitutional Overcorrection

DEFINITION

Restitutional overcorrection means that, when the environment is destroyed or altered, the student must restore it to an improved state.

The notion of restitution is supported by legal and educational institutions. The courts in many states use various forms of restitution in an attempt to pay back the victims of crimes. It is implemented for both major and minor criminal offenses. Thieves are required to repay their victims monetarily, and people who litter may have to spend a certain amount of time picking up litter from streets and highways.

Restitutional overcorrection has appeal in school situations. Normally, when students are punished for disrupting a school environment, they receive their punishment but do not have to take responsibility for their actions. Others clean up the mess that was made by a fight in the hallways. Someone else has to soothe the person who was insulted or harmed by an aggressive classmate. Teachers have to restore peace and quiet to a disturbed learning environment after a student has a tantrum and shouts profanities at others. Restitutional overcorrection seems to serve both as a punishment and as a positive tactic that makes the offender realize the impact of the transgression. When the procedure is applied, the one who destroys or alters an environment must rectify the situation by returning it to an improved state. Foxx and Azrin (1972) pointed out that restitution is best applied immediately after a transgression and should be directly related to the inappropriate act. Burke (1992) provided helpful tips when implementing a restitution intervention:

1. The student who is receiving a restitution intervention should be the one who performed the disruptive behavior as observed by the teacher.

2. The restitution consequence should match the infraction.

3. The student should be expected to perform the restitution even if teacher prompts are necessary.

4. Restitution should not be an activity that the student enjoys. If the student is enjoying the restitution activity, then another intervention is necessary.

In the following example, a principal decided to use restitution with his students.

Several boys were playing in the restroom. As their play became more involved, they smeared liquid soap all over the floors and walls of the lavatory. Paper towels were littered everywhere. The principal, who discovered the boys toward the end of their play, instituted a restitutional overcorrection procedure. He required the boys to completely clean three of the boys' restrooms in the school. They had to clean the walls, mop the floors, and empty all of the litter from each of the restrooms.

Restitutional overcorrection has been used successfully in a number of school situations. In almost all cases, it results in a substantial reduction of undesirable behavior and in a situation that is superior to the one that existed before the incident.

The following are a few examples of cases in which restitution was applied successfully:

1. When the principal caught several students writing graffiti on the walls of the school building, she had them paint all of the walls on that side of the school.

2. When the librarian noticed that a book being returned to the library was defaced with pencil marks, he had the person responsible erase all of the pencil marks in that book, as well as in all books on the first two shelves of the library.

3. Ms. Roberts discovered one of her students writing on his desk. She had him clean all of the desktops in the room.

4. The lunch monitor saw several students littering the remains of their lunches on the floor of the cafeteria. He had them pick up all the litter in the cafeteria and clean the tables during the regular recess period.

5. A student who stole money from another had to pay back her victim with a heavy interest penalty.

These are only a few examples of the application of restitutional overcorrection in school settings. Certainly, the number of applications are almost as infinite as the number of rule violations that can occur at school.

DISCUSSION QUESTIONS

1. How are the recommendations from Foxx and Azrin (1972) and Burke (1992) implemented in the examples listed above?

2. What would be examples of violating Foxx and Azrin's and Burke's recommendations in the examples listed above?

3. What classroom or schoolwide behaviors would be appropriate targets for a restitution intervention?

4. What might be signs of students enjoying a restitution intervention?

5. What might be alternative interventions for students who enjoy the attention of a restitution intervention?

TIPS FOR IMPLEMENTATION

1. Match the type of restitution with the degree of disruption.

2. Implement the restitution immediately following the disruptive behavior.

3. Be sure the student performing the restitution is the one who engaged in the disruptive behavior.

Positive Practice Overcorrection

DEFINITION

Positive practice overcorrection refers to the extreme practice of the desired forms of the target behavior.

The other form of overcorrection, positive practice, has been applied most frequently in special education, although it can be applied to regular education. This procedure requires the students to "overpractice" the desired behavior. An example is taken from a high school setting.

> Mr. Chang's students came into class after period change in a disorderly fashion. They bumped, pushed, shouted, yelled at each other, and wasted a considerable amount of time before settling down to do their assignments. Although he discussed the problem with them on many occasions, their behavior did not improve. He then instituted a positive practice procedure. Each time the class did not enter his room quietly and orderly and did not begin their assignments in the desired fashion, he had the entire class return to the hall and practice the proper way of entering the room. They had to repeat this procedure for 5 minutes.

According to Smith (1989), other examples of positive practice include

1. Holding a hand in the air for 5 minutes due to talking out of turn.

2. Looking up misspelled words in the dictionary for spelling mistakes.

3. Spending recess period practicing quiet transitions for noisy transition periods.

✔ RESEARCH TO PRACTICE.   The power of positive practice was demonstrated in a research study (Azrin & Powers, 1975) in which it was applied to a group who talked out of turn excessively. During the following recess period, the students had to practice raising their hands and obtaining permission to talk without disturbing the others in the class.

TIPS FOR IMPLEMENTATION

1. Keep positive practice sessions between 3 and 5 minutes long.

2. Be sure the practice session focuses on a positive behavior different from the disruptive behavior.

3. Monitor the effectiveness of the intervention.

PRACTICE WHAT YOU'VE LEARNED

1. Identify a behavior for which either restitution or positive practice is appropriate. Design the intervention plan including a data monitoring system.

2. List the pros and cons of restitution and positive practice overcorrection.

3. Discuss ways to pair overcorrection procedures with other interventions previously described.

4. Identify schoolwide behaviors for which overcorrection procedures might be appropriate.

TIMEOUT

Although used by Itard, the teacher of the wild student Victor in the early 1800s (Lane, 1976), timeout did not gain popularity in school settings until the 1970s. It has been used most often in special education. Timeout is the removal of an individual from a situation that is reinforcing and maintaining an inappropriate behavior (Foxx, 1982). Gast and Nelson (1977a, 1977b) delineated three kinds of timeout—contingent observation (discussed in Chapter 3), exclusion timeout, and seclusion timeout—and provided some procedural guidelines for their use.

Exclusion Timeout

DEFINITION

Exclusion timeout means that, upon substantial disruption, the student is excused from class.

When exclusion timeout is implemented, the individual is removed from the situation. Thus, this strategy results in the loss of instructional time, a disadvantage to be considered before using it in a learning situation. The following example shows an effective use of exclusion timeout.

> Juan broke the school lunchroom rules. He tried to initiate a food fight and was too boisterous. The monitor, noticing Juan's infraction, had him leave the lunchroom and remain in the nurse's office the rest of the period.

DISCUSSION QUESTIONS

1. How does the above example illustrate the definition of exclusion timeout?

2. What are other examples of how exclusion timeout can be used?

3. How can exclusion timeout be used at the preschool, elementary, and secondary levels?

4. Why would contingent observation timeout not be the choice of an intervention in the above example?

Seclusion Timeout

DEFINITION

Seclusion timeout means that a pupil who exhibits severe, out-of-control behavior is placed in an isolation room.

When seclusion timeout is used, the student is removed from a situation that is encouraging and maintaining misbehavior and is placed in a situation that is neutral. This type of timeout has received the most publicity and is definitely the most severe form. Most commonly, the student who receives seclusion timeout is placed in a room and isolated from peers and teachers for a designated period of time. Educators must follow many guidelines in considering the use of seclusion timeout. The major guidelines, shown in the checklist of Table 4.1, are discussed in the following sections.

Guidelines for Seclusion Timeout

DOCUMENT OTHER PROCEDURES.   The first thing school personnel should do before implementing seclusion timeout is to document the fact that other procedures (lower on the Intervention Ladder) have been tried without sufficient success. This is important not only to protect school personnel, but also to ensure that students have been given other opportunities to correct their behavior patterns.

TABLE 4.1
Timeout Checklist

Space	Permissions	Data Procedures Planned
___ Always available	___ Principal	___ Data form designed
___ Safe	___ Other appropriate personnel	___ Data form approved by consenting parties
___ At least six feet by six feet		
___ Unlocked	___ Parent(s) or guardian(s) of student	___ Data form posted in convenient place
___ Well lighted		
___ Always supervised		
___ Properly ventilated		

STUDY BEHAVIOR PATTERNS. The students' behavior patterns should be studied by several members of the school staff, who should agree that the disturbing behaviors are severe enough to warrant an intervention that will remove the individual from instruction. Included in this evaluation should be a study of the student's academic work. The teacher must be certain that the student is capable of performing these assignments. If this analysis indicates that the academic work is too difficult and frustrating, the academic assignment should be adjusted first. As discussed in Chapter 2, undesirable social behavior is sometimes a result of frustration with academic tasks.

STUDY THE SITUATION. When considering the use of timeout, a teacher must study the situation from which the pupil will be removed. If, through misbehavior, the student can avoid a difficult assignment, misbehavior will most likely increase rather than decrease.

IDENTIFY APPROPRIATE SPACE. Once pertinent school personnel agree that seclusion timeout should be implemented, an appropriate space must be identified. This space should always be available because, once the procedure is in effect, it must be implemented each and every time the infraction occurs; that is, the use of seclusion timeout must be contingent upon the behavior, not upon the availability of the room or the space. Furthermore, the space should be carefully examined to be certain that it is well ventilated, well lit, safe (the electrical closet will not do), of sufficient size (at least six feet by six feet), not lockable, and always supervised. All of these points are important and should be guaranteed before a room is used for seclusion timeout. The examples below demonstrate the importance of the careful and deliberate selection of space for seclusion timeout.

Mr. Patton could not locate a room for timeout that was near his classroom. In a great stroke of creativity, he decided to "build" his own timeout room in his classroom. As his building supplies, he used the various supply and file cabinets in his room. In essence, he closed off a space along the side of his classroom. After the timeout room was completed, he implemented seclusion timeout for Steve, a student who became easily angered. Mr. Patton did not realize that this space was not safe for Steve or for the others in his class. One time when Steve was sent to timeout, he was especially angry. In a rage, Steve kicked and pounded on the cabinets until one of them toppled over, endangering not only Steve, but those students whose desks were in proximity to the hastily arranged timeout room.

Ms. Wallace decided to use seclusion timeout for one of the girls who liked to swear in class. She could not find a room close to her classroom, but did find a small dressing room near the auditorium that looked suitable. Ms. Wallace explained to Joy what would happen if she swore in class: She would be taken to timeout for 5 minutes. The next time Joy swore in class, Ms. Wallace implemented the procedure, and Joy went to the timeout room. Unfortunately, Ms. Wallace became increasingly busy with her English lesson and forgot about Joy. After a while, Joy locked herself into the dressing room and began to entertain herself. She used the makeup to redecorate the walls and then became bored and angry. She destroyed several costumes and other items that had been left in the dressing room.

These two examples illustrate some of the reasons why the selection of a proper space for seclusion timeout is vital to the safety and security of all involved. Rooms must be supervised, for the potential risks are obvious.

IDENTIFY A TIME FRAME.   In determining the length of time a student should spend in timeout, educators need to keep in mind some valuable research. A discussion of this research follows.

✔ RESEARCH TO PRACTICE.   In an early study of seclusion timeout, White, Nielsen, and Johnson (1972) found that timeouts of short duration are sufficient to produce the desired results. For students who have not previously been exposed to a long seclusion timeout, a period from 1 to 5 minutes is effective.

Because of the advisability of short timeout periods, many teachers use an *extension/release clause* or *changeover delay procedure*, which extends the timeout for 15-second intervals. If the individual is still engaging in misconduct when the timeout period is scheduled to conclude, it is extended for additional 15-second intervals until the student is acting correctly. This procedure ensures that the timeout is as brief as possible, yet indicates to the student that inappropriate behavior in timeout is unacceptable. In Joy's example, the use of a contingent release clause would have helped prevent the unfortunate result of the timeout. The timeout period would have been short, someone would have been supervising her, and school property would not have been destroyed.

INFORM PEOPLE AND OBTAIN PERMISSION.   Because of the potential hazards involved with timeout and the removal of a student from instruction, permission for its use should be obtained and a variety of people must be informed of its implementation. The school administration should be aware of every student who is scheduled for a timeout intervention. One way to

guarantee this knowledge is to obtain signed permissions. The student's parent or guardian should also be aware that the student's school behavior problem is severe enough to warrant this tactic. If nothing else, this process requires some communication between home and school.

KEEP RECORDS. When the decision is made to use timeout, when an appropriate and available room is located, and when all parties agree to its use, the teacher should maintain records about the implementation of this strategy, perhaps with a data sheet (see the sample form shown in Figure 4.2). Whatever record-keeping system is devised, at a minimum it should include (a) a record of each application of timeout, (b) the reason for its

TIMEOUT RECORD-KEEPING FORM

Date	Student's Name	Infraction	Time entered timeout	Time left timeout	Description of behavior in timeout	Educator	Comments
2/5	Paul	Threatening statment	10:05	10:08	swore during 1st minute	DDS	quiet when left
2/5	Tracie	refused to do work	11:15	11:17	quiet	MF	

FIGURE 4.2.   Sample data-keeping form for timeout.

application, and (c) the amount of time spent in seclusion. The record sheet should be posted in a convenient place, possibly near the door of the timeout room. A pencil should be kept nearby so the task of recording data is neither time-consuming nor difficult.

Despite the concerns raised in this discussion of timeout, it is a viable and effective intervention for use at school and, when carefully applied, can result in an improved learning environment for the entire class. Certainly, it is a much more positive intervention than the two remaining on the Intervention Ladder (punishment and exclusion). Bacon (1990) and Burke (1992) offered suggestions for administering timeout procedures, which are found in the "Tips" section.

TIPS FOR IMPLEMENTATION

1. Limit seclusion time.

2. Provide positive reinforcement for alternative behaviors.

3. Avoid overusing timeout.

4. Be sure the behavior that caused the timeout procedure is clear to the student.

5. Provide a warning prior to implementing timeout procedures.

6. Avoid lectures before or after timeout procedures.

PRACTICE WHAT YOU'VE LEARNED

1. Identify behaviors for which exclusion or seclusion timeout may be appropriate.

2. Discuss information that should be shared with parents, students, and administrators prior to implementing timeout procedures in a classroom.

3. Share experiences using exclusion and seclusion timeout procedures, including advantages and disadvantages.

4. List behaviors for which exclusion or seclusion timeout procedures would probably be inappropriate.

PUNISHMENT

DEFINITION

Punishment is the application of an aversive event after an occurrence of an undesired behavior.

Although well grounded in the history of educational practices, punishment should be used only rarely in school settings. One can still hear school board members and some school administrators voicing the old saying, "Spare the rod and spoil the student," but most educators have moved toward a more positive approach to discipline. Clearly, we emphasize the positive approach in this text; the reader merely needs to examine the Intervention Ladder to see that most of the interventions listed are positive in nature (one could even argue the positive aspects of fines, overcorrection, and timeout). Thus, in this section, we primarily include information about why *not* to use punishment in school settings.

Technically, punishment is the application of an aversive event that functionally causes a reduction in the target behavior. Due to its expediency, punishment has been used by parents and teachers to modify children's behavior. Punishment does cause a quick reduction in the target behavior and serves to demonstrate the adult's power and authority (Heron, 1978; Smith, Polloway, & West, 1979), but that power and authority are established through a negative method. Punishment might teach individuals what not to do, but it neither teaches the correct way of behaving (Axelrod & Apsche, 1983; Dreikurs & Grey, 1970) nor establishes respect.

Side Effects of Punishment

Several important side effects of using punishment must be recognized and considered before any adult employs this tactic.

1. Students often associate the punishment with the person who administers it. How can a teacher build a strong relationship with students to encourage learning when they associate that teacher with an aversive event?

2. The student–teacher relationship will be altered after severe punishment, increasing the likelihood that the student will avoid the situation or person administering the punishment. This can result in a student's trying to escape from the school

setting by being truant, skipping classes, or not paying attention, thus impairing conditions for learning.

3. Punishment tends not to generalize; it seems to be specific to the situation in which it is applied. Therefore, it will have to be used in each setting in which the undesirable behavior occurs. As a result, punishment must be used many times to achieve the desired result—the total elimination of the conduct problem.

4. It is not a behavior-building technique. It serves only to reduce a specific behavior and does not teach corollary positive alternatives.

✔ **RESEARCH TO PRACTICE.**   Other negative aspects of punishment have been noted by researchers and scholars. Risley (1968), for example, found that when he used punishment, the undesirable target behavior was reduced in frequency, but another equally undesirable behavior took its place. There might by a "symptom substitution" problem associated with the use of punishment. If this is true, there is little purpose in punishing one behavior only to have another one appear that will have to be punished in turn.

Hewett (1980) proposed that the use of punishment produces an atmosphere of fear. Students either respond because they are afraid not to or do not respond because they are afraid to engage in some behavior. A climate of fear is, of course, not conducive to learning. Optimal learning occurs when students are not afraid to discover, challenge, explore, and expand their thinking by offering new and different ideas.

GUIDELINES FOR PUNISHMENT

1. Punishment should be used only when the behavior is very serious or dangerous.

2. Other tactics should be tried first.

3. Although parental permission is not required for most forms of punishment, Repp and Deitz (1978) suggested that it be granted in writing before the technique occurs so the student will understand why and when punishment will be used.

4. If the behavior does occur, no threats or warnings should be given.

5. The behavior should be stopped as soon as it is noticed.

6. The behavior should be punished each and every time it occurs.

7. The punishment should be of substantial and uniform intensity (it is best not to use mild forms and then gradually increase the intensity).

8. Other positive behaviors of the student should be reinforced. When punishment is used, it should not be the only intervention in effect; there also should be positive elements of the program.

As a result of professional concern about the use of punishment, many state laws and school regulations govern its use. Educators should find out what their own school board and state rulings are concerning the use of punishment before applying it. Recent Supreme Court rulings acknowledge that schools serve an *in loco parentis* role and, therefore, have the constitutional right to employ some corporal punishment. However, the Court makes clear that abuses in this area may subject school personnel to civil actions or criminal actions under state law, as well as civil rights actions under federal law (*Goss v. Lopez*, 1975; *Ingraham v. Wright*, 1977; *Wood v. Strickland*, 1975). Of course, punishment need not take the form of corporal punishment, as any aversive event that serves to reduce a behavior is technically punishment. Regardless of its form, however, if adhered to exclusively, punishment will not lead to a positive school atmosphere.

PRACTICE WHAT YOU'VE LEARNED

1. Describe behaviors for which punishment may be an appropriate intervention.

2. Discuss interventions that could be paired with punishment.

3. List the cautions regarding punishment.

4. Identify and discuss the regulations regarding the use of punishment in your school district.

5. Explain the inappropriate uses of punishment and identify alternative interventions.

EXCLUSION

> The right to attend school is not absolute. It is conditioned on each student's acceptance of the obligation to abide by the lawful rules of the school community until and unless the rules are changed through lawful process. (New Mexico State Department of Education, 1981, p. 2)

Most states use this general reasoning to reserve the right to deny school access to certain regular as well as special education students. Exclusion is a very serious intervention, for it denies students the opportunity for class

attendance and participation in learning experiences. When any of the forms of exclusion are used, the student is not allowed to attend class for some designated period of time. There are three forms of exclusion: *in-school supervision, suspension,* and *expulsion.* Each state differs in its regulations about exclusion; therefore, educators should become fully aware of the specific regulations of their state education agency before considering any of these tactics. The following discussion, then, is general.

In-School Supervision

DEFINITION

In-school supervision means that a student is removed from one or more classes and required to spend the time in a designated school area.

GUIDELINES FOR IN-SCHOOL SUPERVISION.   In-school supervision, the mildest form of exclusion, requires a permanent room and a supervisor. When this tactic is scheduled, an individual who breaks a school or classroom rule is removed for one or more classes and spends that time in a designated school area. Because students miss class, this intervention is usually reserved for major disruptive acts, such as fighting or frequent tardiness (Emmer, Evertson, Sanford, Clements, & Worsham, 1984). During in-school supervision, students are denied all school privileges, spend their time completing school work, and are prohibited from talking (Bacon, 1990). This tactic (which could be considered a form of exclusion timeout) has been used successfully in many middle and secondary schools. In-school supervision procedures can be successful if the following guidelines are followed:

1. It is implemented consistently across the entire school.

2. One supervised place is designated for supervision, freeing teachers from having to make their own special arrangements.

3. The in-school supervision room should not be considered by the students as a better place to be than class. If it is less aversive to go to the in-school supervision room than class, then many will purposely be tardy to avoid a more unpleasant situation.

The following example illustrates in-school supervision guidelines. The example comes from one high school that had a chronic problem with tardiness to classes after each period change.

> Ms. Brown, principal at Leigh High School, was aware of a serious problem during period changes. Students wandered around the hallways, and many were very late to their classes. Teachers reported that some were 15 minutes late to class, and many straggled in at random times. This was very disruptive to the teachers and to students who had already begun their assignments. Ms. Brown decided to implement an in-school supervision procedure. She designated one room for this purpose and assigned an aide for supervision. Once the second bell rang, all those still in the hallways and not in their assigned classrooms were sent to the in-school supervision room for the remainder of that period. Various seatwork assignments were given to the students who had missed their classes. In addition, they were given a make-up assignment for the work they had missed in class. Soon tardiness was reduced to a minimum.

DISCUSSION QUESTIONS

1. How are the guidelines for in-school supervision followed in the above example?

2. What are the advantages of the in-school supervision procedure?

3. What cautions must be considered regarding in-school supervision?

BENEFITS OF IN-SCHOOL SUPERVISION.   In general, an in-school supervision room has many benefits. It provides teachers with a place to send those students who are so disruptive that they will not allow their classmates to learn. When such an arrangement is provided, teachers do not have to miss their own lunch breaks, planning periods, or free periods to supervise disorderly students. This is a great benefit to many teachers who are busy, need their free time for planning, and are reluctant to lose that time because of the conduct problems of the few.

In-school supervision has benefits for students as well. They are required to complete school work, and in some cases are given additional work to finish. Students are in school rather than out on the streets if parental supervision is not available during the day. Finally, the in-school supervision procedure, if implemented correctly, should serve as a deterrent to future disruptive acts that resulted in the intervention in the first place.

Suspension

DEFINITION

Suspension is the removal of an individual from school for a specified number of days, not usually longer than 10 school days.

Expulsion

DEFINITION

Expulsion is the removal of a student from school either permanently or for an indefinite time, usually exceeding 10 school days.

Suspension and expulsion are very serious forms of exclusion, and the full ramifications of their influence must be considered before they are implemented. These forms of exclusion have received attention in the literature due to their seriousness and potential ramifications (Bartlett, 1989; Rose, 1988; Yell, 1989). Suspension results in a person's being removed from school for a period of time, not usually longer than 10 school days. Expulsion requires the individual to be denied access to school for some period of time longer than 10 days, often indefinitely.

GUIDELINES FOR SUSPENSION AND EXPULSION

1. Official notice and some kind of hearing must be given before either tactic is used.

2. In emergency situations, a student may be removed from school without a prior hearing for a maximum of one school day.

3. A postsuspension hearing must be held as soon as possible. The constitutionally required formality of these hearings var-

ies, so it is important to follow state and local regulations precisely regarding their implementation.

4. Parents are entitled to a written statement citing reasons for the suspension.

5. Parents must be notified of their rights to due process.

6. When students' behaviors result from disabilities, they cannot be suspended or expelled pending additional findings by the staffing committee. Generally, the question is whether there is any educational procedure that can address the problem.

7. The decision cannot be affected by whether the school currently has an appropriate program available or whether the school personnel desire to address the problem.

DISADVANTAGES OF SUSPENSION AND EXPULSION. The seriousness of these interventions cannot be overstated. Although each temporarily rids the school of the problem, it rarely serves as a remediation procedure. Most students who are seriously disobedient at school are not succeeding at school either academically or socially. For them, a bona fide reason not to go to school can serve as a reinforcer. They can escape an unpleasant experience with the blessings of school personnel. This is one reason suspension often results in ensuing suspensions.

Another reason for this cycle also stems from the reinforcement paradigm. Once outside the constraints of the school day, many of these students find activities that are fun, exciting, and often free from adult authority. They can watch television, play arcade games, wander the streets, or interact with gang members. In many cases, they can develop a set of friends outside the school environment who encourage reckless and even lawless behaviors. Basically, educators who use suspension and expulsion are giving up on the student, indicating that they cannot control or educate this individual. Before such measures are employed, school personnel should have tried other interventions on the Intervention Ladder.

School administrators must be aware of the different rules, regulations, and procedures that apply specifically to special education students. This is particularly necessary when exclusion is being considered. If students have been placed in special education because of serious behavior problems, they cannot be removed from school because of them. In short, administrators must be knowledgeable about the rules and regulations that could influence their decisions about the appropriateness of specific interventions with particular populations of the school community.

DISCUSSION QUESTIONS

1. What are the suspension and expulsion guidelines in your school?

2. How are suspension and expulsion decisions made?

3. What behaviors warrant suspension and expulsion in your school?

4. How are parents involved in the process?

5. How are students involved in the process?

6. What alternative interventions are usually tried before suspension or expulsion?

INVOLVEMENT OF LAW ENFORCEMENT AGENCIES

The last intervention discussed in this chapter does not appear on the Intervention Ladder for it is one that school officials usually avoid. Schools are often worlds in themselves where students are free from criminal prosecution. Where else can people assault others and not be prosecuted by the law? Where else can they steal, destroy property, vandalize, and victimize without the worry of an encounter with law enforcement officials? Many students are aware of their protection and abuse it. One example from a school situation illustrates this point.

> In most states, school officials have the right to search and seize property without permission or a warrant. This was the case in one high school in which administrators heard a rumor that weapons were being kept in school lockers. One morning, the principal and several other school administrators opened all of the lockers in the school. They found an arsenal of knives, shotguns, and various handguns, complete with ammunition. They made the decision not to inform the law authorities or the press, and had the students remove the weapons from school property. They made this decision although they knew that students had violated state and local laws regarding concealed weapons and the requirements for permits to have these arms.

One reason these school administrators decided not to contact law enforcement agencies was that they wanted to protect these youth from criminal prosecution. In that state, the alternatives for those breaking the law are bleak. Seldom does criminal prosecution result in remedial or educational programming. With the best interests of the students in mind, administrators decided to handle the problem internally. Hobbs (1975) probably would have applauded the actions of these school officials. He felt that labeling a student as a juvenile delinquent (the consequence of criminal prosecution) actually changes the way that individual is perceived by society and himself or herself. Society views that individual with distrust and suspicion, and he or she tends to seek friends who also have been so labeled. Once this occurs, the person seeks the approval and recognition of others already acting outside of socially appropriate channels. Hobbs claimed that "through interaction with students who have learned to survive as delinquents, he will learn delinquent attitudes, antisocial feelings, and techniques of crime. He will become more fundamentally what he has been defined as being" (p. 150).

The involvement of law enforcement agencies has serious implications for all parties involved. Clearly, unless there are state laws or school board regulations on the issue, the question whether to report an incident is within the administrator's discretion. The following questions should be considered before a decision is made:

1. Was the behavior a danger to other students or staff?

2. Has the student exhibited other dangerous behaviors in the past?

3. Is this likely to occur in the future?

4. Is this a behavior the school is capable of addressing?

If the behavior puts the safety of others in jeopardy and if school personnel cannot control the student, school administrators should consider handling criminal offenses as the nonschool community does.

Until the criminal justice system can arrange alternative ways to deal with minors who break laws, it is probably best to keep as many students as possible from the law enforcement system as long as possible. Even though many school officials follow this advice, it seems important to instill in disobedient youth the awareness that they have seriously violated school rules and criminal laws. Whoever deals with these infractions must apply consequences for these actions. Otherwise, more serious events may occur because students come to believe that, while on school grounds, they are protected from the rules and laws that exist elsewhere.

SUMMARY

In this chapter,

1. Interventions found on the upper part of the Intervention Ladder were discussed.

2. These procedures ranged from simple to relatively complex interventions.

3. Whenever possible, interventions from this portion of the ladder should be paired with interventions from the lower part.

4. Interventions found on the upper part of the ladder tend to be necessary for fewer students and require more direct teacher time.

As a review and summary, Table 4.2 presents a list of these interventions, along with the definition and an example of each.

CHAPTER DISCUSSION ACTIVITIES

1. What are some reasons for using interventions from the upper part of the ladder?

2. Discuss examples of difficult or more punitive forms of direct intervention.

3. How and when are difficult or more punitive forms of interventions implemented?

4. Cite research that exists to support the efficacy of the interventions.

5. What are examples of when to use the interventions?

BEHAVIORS AND INTERVENTIONS

1. Discuss specific behaviors from your own experience that might be addressed by interventions described in this chapter. Identify interventions from the lower part of the Intervention Ladder that could be used concurrently with interventions from this chapter to change student behavior.

2. Discuss some of the sociological factors that have a direct bearing on school discipline. Describe some interventions that could be useful to address these factors.

TABLE 4.2
Glossary for the Intervention Ladder, Part 2

Tactic	Definition	Example
PEER MANAGEMENT		
Tutoring	One student proficient in an academic assignment serves in the role of teacher for a classmate who needs additional assistance.	Sally had difficulty learning her arithmetic facts and, therefore, was very disruptive during the time scheduled for arithmetic. Her teacher paired her with a classmate for extra drill and practice, which resulted in less disruption and Sally's mastery of arithmetic facts.
Behavioral managers	One whose classroom behavior is usually appropriate earns the privilege of becoming the dispenser of praise and rewards for a peer.	After training in behavioral techniques, Brian became the behaviorial manager for Kevin. Brian modeled correct behavior and reinforced Kevin when he acted appropriately.
Environmental restructuring	The class is instructed and reinforced for encouraging a classmate's appropriate behavior.	Franklin had a history of disturbing class during study and seatwork assignments. In the past, the class laughed at Franklin and encouraged his disruption. After discussion and training sessions, the class learned to praise his quiet working behavior and ignore his disruptions.
SELF-MANAGEMENT		
Self-regulation	Individuals monitor their own behavior, seek to avoid those situations that precipitate inappropriate behavior, and stop that behavior if it is initiated.	When Bill realized that he and Lonnie were about to begin to fight, Bill left the playground and returned to his classroom.
Self-evaluation	Correcting one's own performance, recording the frequency, and graphing the resulting data.	Judy marked each time she talked out during school on a score sheet kept on her desk. At the end of each day, she totaled the tallies and graphed the score.

(continued)

TABLE 4.2
Continued

Tactic	Definition	Example
Self-reinforcement	Rewarding oneself for correct behavior.	Because Leroy did not get into trouble that day in the lunchroom, he stopped at a convenience store after school and treated himself to a soda.
OVERCORRECTION Positive practice	Extreme practice of the desired forms of the target behavior.	Megin pushed and shoved her way into class after recess. For the next 5 school days, she had to hold the classroom door open for her classmates. This made her the last one returning to class after recess and lunch breaks.
Restitution	When the environment is destroyed or altered, the student must restore it to an improved state.	In a mood of defiance, Gail tipped over her desk. As her consequence, she had to straighten the entire classroom.
Exclusion	Upon substantial disruption, the student is excused from class.	Sarah was too noisy during music, so the music teacher had her return to her homeroom.
Seclusion	For severe, out-of-control behavior, the pupil is placed in an isolation room.	Whenever John had a violent temper tantrum, he was sent to a timeout room for a minimum of 3 minutes.
PUNISHMENT	The application of an aversive event after an occurrence of an undesired behavior.	Nancy had to stay after school, and the teacher doubled the amount of homework for refusing to do her seatwork assignment.
EXCLUSION In-school supervision	Removal of a student from one or more classes while requiring him or her to spend the time in a designated school area.	After considerable unruly and disruptive conduct in Algebra and English, Mary Jane was assigned to spend that time in the counselor's office for 3 school days.

(continued)

TABLE 4.2
Continued

Tactic	Definition	Example
Suspension	The removal of an individual from school for a specified number of days, not usually longer than 10 school days.	After a variety of interventions were scheduled unsuccessfully and a hearing was held, Nathan was suspended for 1 week because he defiantly disobeyed his teachers, destroyed school property, and threatened other students.
Expulsion	Removal of a student from school either permanently or for an indefinite time, usually exceeding 10 school days.	School personnel had tried all means available to them to control Mark's conduct. Despite their attempts, Mark fought with other students, threatened his teachers, and destroyed the learning environment for his classmates. After a formal hearing, Mark was expelled from school for a month.

3. Describe a plan using interventions from Chapters 3 and 4 to address the following behaviors:

- Chronic tardiness

- Fighting

- Possession of a weapon

- Possession of drugs

- Smoking

- Hitting a teacher

- Threatening a student

- Theft

- Truancy

- Cutting classes

- Defacing property

- Pushing and shoving

- Difficulty completing work
- Difficulty working independently
- Difficulty staying on task
- Fighting on the playground
- Problems in the hall
- Talking out
- Bothering neighbors
- Temper tantrums
- Lying
- Wetting pants
- Vandalism
- Gang behavior
- Insubordination

5

Evaluation

OBJECTIVES

After reading this chapter, you should be able to

1. Describe behaviors to be measured.

2. Explain ways to measure behaviors.

3. Identify when behaviors should be measured.

4. Discuss who should conduct the measurement.

5. Explain measurement systems.

6. Describe evaluation phases.

7. Record data.

8. Participate in "Practice What You've Learned" activities.

Evaluation ideas to be discussed in this chapter include

- **What Should Be Measured?**
- **How Should Behavior Be Measured?**
- **When Should Behavior Be Measured?**
- **Who Should Conduct the Measurements?**
- **Measurement Systems**
- **Evaluation Phases**
- **Displaying Data**

n the previous two chapters, we presented a variety of proven intervention procedures for modifying disruptive and disobedient behaviors. One major theme of those chapters was to use tactics lower on the Intervention Ladder first. More stringent procedures should be selected only when less intrusive techniques are not sufficiently powerful to change the target behavior to meet the requirements of desired school and classroom deportment. The following questions then arise: How do I know if the procedures I implemented are working? How do I communicate the effects of those intervention procedures to other educators, parents, and the student? The primary purposes of this chapter are to give educators guidelines for conducting evaluation concurrent with implementing intervention techniques and a format for data presentation that is easily and readily communicated. The evaluation methods discussed here are simple but powerful enough for the purposes of judging the effectiveness of intervention procedures and communicating those effects to others.

WHAT SHOULD BE MEASURED?

The behaviors that are of utmost concern should be the targets of the measurement. In other words, the measurement should focus directly on the behaviors that the educator seeks to change. In many cases, this consists of a number of behaviors that form a category. For example, Tom has a reputation for being aggressive. Aggression can consist of many different behaviors. Some people are aggressive verbally, whereas others are aggressive physically. Some students' physical aggression takes the form of fighting; others pull hair, bite, kick, and pinch other students. Before the effects of any intervention can be measured, the educator must determine the target behavior, precisely define what is to be modified, and thereby identify what is to be measured.

The behavior targeted for remediation must be defined carefully in observable terms. It must be something that can be consistently observed over a period of time. Moods, feelings, and self-concepts are very difficult to measure in this way. However, inappropriate behaviors resulting from underlying psychological constructs are within the teacher's and counselor's abilities to measure and change. For example, Susan is said to be "moody," but when she is in a bad mood she verbally assaults her classmates and teachers. Those verbal assaults include talking back to her teachers, swearing at her classmates, and announcing that she will not do her work or follow classroom rules. For a successful behavior program to be implemented, the last three rather specific behaviors should be targeted; as they improve, so will moodiness. Educators frequently report that the by-products of direct intervention on inappropriate school behavior are improved self-concept, more pleasant personality, and a sense of happiness in the student.

Identification of the target behaviors can be easily accomplished by informal observations and anecdotal record keeping. Notes about what specific behaviors comprise disobedient acts can be very helpful in determining exactly what behaviors need remediation. During this observation period, many educators often find that the behaviors of concern are not as pervasive, general, or unmanageable as they had thought. For example, Mr. West's fourth-period class was very disruptive. After careful observation, he discovered that disruption in that class consisted only of talking out of turn and being out of seat. It did not include defiance, physical aggression, joking around, or major acts of disorderly conduct, such as tantrums. Once Mr. West understood what the disruption consisted of, he could more efficiently select an intervention strategy and measure its effectiveness.

This identification period must be complete because its main purpose is to identify what is to be measured. If the educator changes his or her mind in the middle of the evaluation phase, the data gathered become use-

less. If Mr. West begins interventions aimed at reducing being out of seat and talking out of turn and later adds being tardy to class, he will be unable to tell from his evaluation procedures if the intervention he selected was effective. For example, Mr. West might start to evaluate how often students are out of seat and talking out of turn and find that the daily occurrence of these behaviors is 40. He then implements an intervention to reduce the frequency of these behaviors. If the daily behavior record now indicates that the students talked out of turn and were out of seat only four times during fourth period, he would know that his behavioral program was working. However, if at some point during his measurement, he added tardiness to the list of target behaviors and saw a rise in the daily occurrence of disruptions, he would be unable to evaluate accurately the changes resulting from his planned efforts. Of course, he could also begin measuring tardiness, but those data should be kept separate from the first two targets he had already identified and begun to remediate. One key to successful evaluation is consistency in the behaviors measured and the strategy scheduled. Thus, to determine what to measure, educators should

1. Select a behavior that is of great concern (e.g., causing destruction, interfering with instruction, hurting self or another student).

2. Define precisely the behavior to be measured (i.e., must be observable, countable, and have a beginning and end).

3. Observe the behavior consistently over a period of time (i.e., observe at the same time each day, for the same amount of observation time).

HOW SHOULD BEHAVIOR BE MEASURED?

Behavior should be measured in the simplest way possible and with as much immediacy as possible. Although evaluations of intervention programs can become terribly complex, there is no need for this complexity. Evaluation of a behavioral intervention is not inherently better because it took hours to complete and involved an unwieldy measurement system requiring outside data takers. Often, the simpler system results in easier application and communication. Therefore, only uncomplicated measurement or evaluation methods are discussed in this chapter.

Once the behavior or set of behaviors to be targeted for remediation are identified precisely, the teacher or counselor must decide what measurement system to use to determine the success of the intervention procedure selected. The measurement system selected depends directly on the

type of behavior change the educator desires. Is the educator concerned with the amount or *frequency* of the behavior or with the *duration* of the behavior? For example, the amount or frequency of the following behaviors is usually what constitutes the problem: litter on school grounds, defacement or destruction of property, talking back to the teacher, homework assignments not completed and turned in, seatwork assignments not completed, or library books not returned. However, for some behaviors, educators are more concerned about the duration of the target behavior: the amount of time wasted during class, the amount of time required to prepare for leaving school at the end of the day, or the amount of time spent moving from the school bus to the classroom.

In some cases, both the frequency and the duration of the behavior can be of concern. In these situations, the educator should decide which aspect is more important (or take both frequency and duration data concurrently). For example, is it more important to reduce the amount of time it takes for students to enter a class and begin work after a period change or to reduce the number of students who are tardy? Examples of behaviors for which either frequency or duration might be appropriate measurement systems are out-of-seat behaviors, tantrums or acts of violence (e.g., fighting), tardiness, and talking out of turn. The frequency and duration of these behaviors are not necessarily dependent on each other. Ms. Harris's biology lab students were usually very late and disorderly. She attempted to reduce the number of late students each day, but found that the amount of time wasted due to tardiness did not decrease sufficiently. Although the number of students who were tardy decreased, the few who continued to be tardy were as late as they were before Ms. Harris implemented her intervention. Therefore, she changed her measurement system so that it was sensitive to the amount of each lab period wasted due to tardiness and delay in beginning the assignment.

The same phenomenon applies to many other commonly targeted behaviors. Mr. VanEtten wanted to modify Carlene's out-of-seat behavior. He decided to measure the frequency with which Carlene left her seat and wandered around the room during seatwork assignments. Although her frequency of out-of-seat behavior dropped from about 15 occurrences for each daily seatwork assignment session to two during intervention, she was still very distracting to the teacher and the rest of the class because, although the frequency of the target behavior decreased to a reasonable number, the duration did not. She spent most of the class period wandering around the room, never returning to her desk. It became clear that Mr. VanEtten had to change the duration of the target behavior without allowing its frequency to return to the previous level. Thus, when determining how to measure behavior,

1. Use the simplest technique.

2. Select a system that is sensitive to the target behavior.

WHEN SHOULD BEHAVIOR BE MEASURED?

Behavior should be measured in the same way and at the same time each day that the educator and student work together. For example, Mr. VanEtten should measure Carlene's out-of-seat behavior when seatwork assignments are scheduled. Although he assigns seatwork several times during the school day, he always schedules seatwork from 10:15 to 11:00 daily and might decide to use this period for measuring the frequency of Carlene's out-of-seat episodes. In this way, he collects data at a consistent time each day.

The notion of consistent and daily (or very frequent) applications of intervention and measurement systems is important. The purpose of collecting precise information about student performance is to determine whether the infraction is serious and whether the intervention scheduled causes the desired improvement. To judge the effectiveness of the intervention, the educator must be able to compare one day's performance with another and one week's performance with that of the ensuing week. For this to occur, the measures of the target behavior must be equivalent. They must be taken on the same behavior or set of behaviors, they must be measured with the same measurement system, and they must be taken under similar conditions. Otherwise, comparisons and overall evaluations are impossible.

In addition, the measurement should be frequent. Whenever possible, the intervention should be applied each day and its effectiveness evaluated daily. If a high school student who is receiving an intervention program is supposed to attend the teacher's class only three times each week, the teacher should apply the planned intervention and measure its effectiveness during each of the three periods. If cleanliness in the restrooms is targeted for remediation, then the janitor, principal, or other designated person should evaluate the state of the restrooms on a daily basis and as precisely as possible (e.g., number of items littered or number of clean sinks).

Educators need frequent information about the effectiveness of their programs for several reasons. First, frequent measurements provide an accurate and complete picture of the student's behavior patterns. In this way, educators can assess the seriousness and pervasiveness of the infraction. Some rule violations are serious but do not occur often. For example, Tanis breaks school windows only twice a month, whereas Dan drops a chewing gum wrapper on school grounds daily. Infrequent observations yield an incomplete picture that is more difficult to understand and communicate to others. Second, educators need to know as soon as possible whether the

programs they have put into operation are producing the intended results. Particularly for serious infractions, educators must know as quickly as possible whether improvement is noted. Pre- and posttesting with several months between each evaluation is a luxury that educators and school environments cannot afford. Third, it is important for subsequent educational planning that information be readily available. If an intervention low on the Intervention Ladder does not produce the desired results, other procedures must be implemented. The only way to judge whether more stringent procedures are necessary is to know within a short period of time whether less intrusive interventions have worked. Thus, when deciding when behavior should be measured, the educator should

1. Utilize the measurement the same way and same time each day.

2. Select a consistent time daily to measure the behavior.

3. Compare the data from one day and week to the next.

4. Measure frequently, preferably daily.

WHO SHOULD CONDUCT THE MEASUREMENTS?

There is no mystique about measuring student performance or collecting data on students' school behavior. Once the target behavior has been identified, the proper measurement system selected, and the time period for measurement determined, the collection and display of the evaluation data are relatively simple. With some initial guidance and periodic monitoring, practically anyone can be assigned the task of collecting the data upon which evaluation decisions will be made.

Typically, the adult in charge of the situation in which student behavior is measured is the one who conducts the measurement. In other words, the classroom teacher concerned about deportment defines the set of target behaviors, collects the daily information about that performance, and evaluates it in relation to the intervention strategies implemented. The playground supervisor monitors the number of fights and other disturbances that occur during recess. The adult supervising the cafeteria counts the number of instances in which litter is inappropriately disposed of after each lunch period. The bus driver keeps a tally of the number of major disturbances during the ride to and from school. Although these tasks are most often carried out by these adults, the duties can be viewed as an extra burden on the already busy adult.

Many other people can collect data on student performance. Both experience and research indicate that people other than teachers can collect accurate information. A student can earn the privilege of keeping a record of the number of rule infractions by classmates for a week if he or she meets a set criterion for good classroom deportment. Dependable students can be used to collect behavioral data in a variety of settings: the school bus, the halls, the playground, assemblies, the cafeteria, and the classroom. The measurement systems described in the next section are simple enough that students may assume the responsibilities of collecting the data, thus freeing the teacher for more important tasks such as instruction.

The target individuals also are good resources for collecting behavioral information. As discussed in Chapter 4, students who monitor their own behavior often make gains far greater than those who are evaluated by teachers or other adults. When these students are asked to keep records of their own performance, their performance often improves without additional intervention strategies. Because of this research finding, teachers should attempt to have target students monitor their own behaviors by collecting daily data on their infractions. Of course, the teacher must monitor such situations to ensure that the students accurately record their own behavior. Many stu-

dents initially need assistance so they will be neither too stringent nor too lenient on themselves.

The school day is already filled with many noninstructional tasks, and teachers' time is consumed with activities that limit their abilities to concentrate on instruction. The elimination or reduction of various behavioral distractions will result in increased instructional time, but teachers do not have to spend their time collecting information about deportment. The students can do that for themselves. Thus, individuals who should conduct the measurement include

1. Teacher

2. Student

3. Educational assistant

MEASUREMENT SYSTEMS

Many measurement systems can be used for evaluating the effectiveness of intervention procedures on the improvement of student performance. Some of these (e.g., correct and error rate scores, percentage correct scores) are applicable mainly to instructional situations. Because this book centers on the amelioration of behavior problems, we do not discuss those measurement systems. Rather, we include only simple data collection systems that provide information about the improvement of discipline problems. The two measurement systems that are most useful assess frequency and duration.

Frequency as a measure of students' responses is simply an indication of how many times the student engages in the target behavior. It is a tally of the number of times the behavior occurs over a constant period of time, or how many students engage in the target behavior. For example, one data collector found that, on Tuesday, Todd turned in *five* pages of completed homework assignments. Another found that *fifteen* students came to fifth-period English class on time. Whoever is in charge of collecting the data merely keeps a count.

The collection of frequency data is not difficult. During the time period in which data are to be collected, the data collector merely tallies each time the target behavior occurs. Some teachers tape an index card on a top corner of the pupil's desk and instructs the student to make a mark each time an infraction is observed. Other teachers use a reverse counting system, such as the one used by Sulzbacher and Houser (1968). With this system, the teacher uses a flip chart or writes a series of numbers on the blackboard. Each time an infraction occurs, the "score" is reduced by a point. For example, if the class can earn 5 minutes of free time at the end of the period

as a reward for not violating any rules, then the teacher would write the numbers from 5 to 0 on the blackboard or on separate cards of a flip chart. Whenever an infraction is observed, the teacher erases the highest number on the blackboard or flips a card to reveal the next lower number. At the end of the period, the students know how many minutes of free time the class has earned, and the teacher knows how many rule infractions occurred that period. That daily score should be entered on a raw data sheet (described later), which serves as a permanent record of the number of infractions for that period.

Duration data are also easy to keep. They answer the question "How much time did the student engage in a certain activity?" How long did

Jeremy wander around the room? How long did it take the class to begin assignments after the period change?

To collect these data, the teacher or assigned data collector should be given a stopwatch that can accumulate time. When the behavior under consideration begins, the stopwatch is started. When the episode is concluded, the stopwatch is stopped. At the end of the period, the total amount of time spent in the target behavior appears on the face of the stopwatch. When this method of collecting duration data is used, the teacher knows the total time that a student engaged in the undesirable behavior for the observation period, not how long each episode lasted. However, because the major concern is the total amount of instructional time being misused, information about each occurrence of the target behavior during the period is not as important. For those who want information about each occurrence during an observation period, a written notation of the time taken for each episode must be made; however, this procedure is time-consuming and could be very distracting to the instructional situation.

If a stopwatch is not available, a clock with a second hand can be used for collecting duration data. Although this procedure is more awkward, the data collector writes down the start and stop times for each episode. At the end of the period, the daily score is obtained by totaling the time spent in the behavior being monitored. This method provides additional information on frequency and the duration of each occurrence.

As with frequency data, the teacher or data keeper should enter the day's score on an overall record sheet. In this way, a permanent record of each day's data is available for future evaluation.

Percentage of occurrence is a measurement system that adjusts for inconsistent observation times. As mentioned above, if frequency or duration data are collected, the time period for data collection should be constant because the purpose is to compare one day's data with another. In this way, the student's improvement and the intervention procedure's success can be evaluated. The following example should illustrate this point.

> Mr. Lovitt was very concerned about Catherine's defiance. She complained about her assignments, challenged her grades on daily quizzes and seatwork tasks, and refused to do her work. Mr. Lovitt felt that Catherine had a serious attitude problem, which was manifested in her noncompliance in regard to school work. He decided to monitor her behavior. He carefully defined the behaviors that he wanted to measure and decided to use frequency data to evaluate them. During the assessment phase, he recorded the frequency of Catherine's noncompliance for a week and found that the behavior had occurred about 10 times each day during his set observation period. He selected an intervention from the Intervention Ladder and scheduled it for the next week of

school. The occurrences he recorded during the 5 days the intervention was in effect were 10, 7, 5, 8, and 6, or an average of 7 instances daily of noncompliance. Although the daily average from the intervention period was lower than that of the assessment phase, Catherine's behavior did not seem to be improving. Then Mr. Lovitt realized that, due to scheduling difficulties on Tuesday, Wednesday, and Friday, his observation times during the second week had been substantially shorter than the usual 50-minute instructional period. This rendered a comparison of the assessment phase to the intervention phase impossible. He could not even compare individual days during the intervention with each other. He was finally forced to conclude that, when the different lengths of observation times were considered, Catherine's noncompliance had actually increased during the intervention period.

In this example, the teacher could not truly evaluate the effectiveness of his remediation plan because observation times were inconsistent. This situation occurs in many school settings when instructors do not see students for a consistent amount of time each day. Abbreviated school days contribute to this problem. When consistent observation times are not possible on a

TABLE 5.1
Summary of Data Collection Systems

Measurement System	Definition	Formula	Example
Frequency	Number of occurrences; how many times the behavior occurred (session time or the number of opportunities must be held constant)	Count or tally	⊔⊔⊤⊤ 1 = 6
Duration	Total amount of time the behavior lasts; how long the individual engaged in the activity (session time must be held constant)	Cumulative time, time of each episode added together	Stopwatch reading; 16 minutes = 16 Each episode: 5:10, 4:05, 1:15 = 10:30
Percentage of occurrence for frequency	The proportion or ratio between the number of occurrences and the number of opportunities	No. occurrences ÷ no. of opportunities × 100	$15/30 \times 100 = 50\%$
Percentage of occurrence for duration	The proportion or ratio of the amount of time engaged in the behavior for the observation period	No. of minutes engaged in behavior ÷ observation time × 100	$10/40 \times 100 = 25\%$

daily basis, simple frequency and duration data are not useful without an additional calculation. When this situation occurs, the raw data must be turned into percentages. The two formulas provided in the last two rows of Table 5.1 allow for a calculation of percentages from simple frequency and duration data, thereby allowing for comparisons even when the observation time cannot be held constant.

In most school situations, this additional calculation is not necessary. In middle and high schools, academic periods last for a rather consistent length of time. On the rare days when the schedule is altered, those data can be discounted and not entered into the permanent record. Tardiness is usually observed under constant conditions, and simple duration data are sufficient for daily and weekly comparisons. In elementary schools, teachers usually schedule their school day according to a constant set of time periods. Some keep records of school deportment for the entire school day. In these cases, simple frequency and duration data suffice. When daily observation times are inconsistent, however, it is necessary to spend the extra time calculating percentage of occurrence. It should be noted that any percentage scores are somewhat biased by the shorter observation times.

EVALUATION PHASES

Four basic phases should be included in all behavioral evaluation plans: assessment, intervention, maintenance, and follow-up.

Assessment Phase

As discussed earlier, evaluation data should be taken as frequently as possible. This information ideally should be collected each time the educator interacts with the student (e.g., each English period, daily between 9:00 and 10:15, every morning recess period, all lunch breaks in the cafeteria). Although interventions are planned and implemented only when the need is obvious to those educators who work with particular individuals, consistent daily assessment is required before interventions are scheduled. The purpose of this assessment phase is to record the initial performance levels for comparison after the intervention program has begun. However, this phase has many additional benefits. Often, the educator finds that the correct behavior had not been identified. This phase may indicate that what was thought to be the target behavior was not the problem at all and that other behaviors needed to be identified and measured precisely. This assessment phase may reveal the seriousness of the problem and result in selection of a procedure higher on the Intervention Ladder than originally planned. Of course, the primary benefit of the assessment phase is for later comparisons. Only when educators know the original levels of the behavior under consideration can an evaluation or comparison of long- and short-term effects be made.

Intervention Phase

After the assessment period, which rarely needs to be longer than one school week, the selected intervention should be implemented on a daily or frequent schedule. The intervention selected should be in effect each observation day during this phase. After several days of explaining the intervention strategy to the students, the teacher need not provide daily instructions. However, the intervention should be implemented on the standard observation schedule. For example, if the principal, Mr. Mathews, has implemented a restitutional overcorrection intervention and an incentive to encourage students to report offenders to reduce graffiti on the school walls, each day someone must check the walls. If new paintings, drawings, or slogans are located, the reward must be offered to the school population. Once the culprits are found, the intervention must be implemented.

The intervention phase should last as long as necessary. An intervention should be terminated, for example, if the intervention is unsuccessful or if a criterion has been met. The only way these determinations can be made is for data to be readily available. Sometimes an intervention is effective initially, but loses power with time. When the evaluation data indicate that this has occurred, another intervention strategy should be planned that adds to or replaces the first. Unfortunately, not all interventions work as hoped or expected. If evaluation data indicate that the behavior worsened or that the intervention did not produce the desired results, another plan must be put into effect. Therefore, many remediation programs include more than one intervention phase. On the other hand, when the first intervention procedure produces the desired result, the daily application of the intervention may be discontinued.

Maintenance Phase

Unfortunately, when interventions are halted, the previous undesirable behavior patterns often return. Thus, the educator must continue to measure the target behavior for several weeks after the intervention phase is concluded according to the schedule followed during the assessment and intervention conditions. If the desired deportment is maintained, then periodic checks should ensue; however, if the behavior pattern deteriorates, the intervention should be implemented again. Reinstituting the successful plan for a longer period of time often produces the desired long-term results.

Sometimes, however, other interventions (e.g., parent involvement, self-management) need to be put into effect. Regardless, without complete and continuing evaluation, educators have limited information upon which to act.

Follow-Up Phase

The last phase of every behavioral project should be periodic follow-up. Once each week, perhaps on random days, the targeted behavior is monitored to ensure that maintenance continues. If behavior worsens, remediation procedures can be implemented early to avoid the possibility of the behavior's returning to the initial intolerable levels that made intervention necessary in the first place. Figure 5.1 displays a typical format for graphing the entire evaluation process, including the separate phases.

When designing an intervention plan for a targeted behavior, the educator should

1. Conduct an assessment phase (baseline) to obtain information about initial performance.

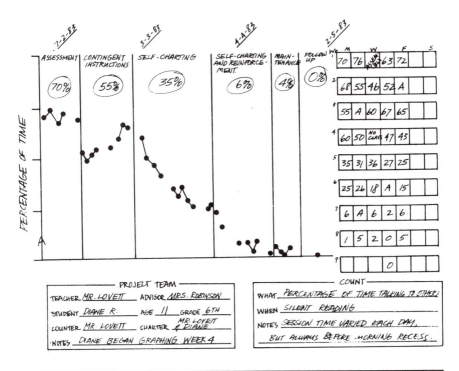

FIGURE 5.1. Sample evaluation graph.

2. Select a measurement system that is sensitive to the targeted behavior.

3. Measure daily at the same time of day.

4. Examine the assessment phase data to determine an appropriate intervention. There should be a good match between infraction and intervention.

5. Implement the intervention systematically daily.

6. Establish a criterion for mastery.

7. Compare daily data with assessment phase data to determine if progress is being made with the targeted behavior.

8. Conduct periodic checks to ascertain that the criterion level is maintained.

9. Intervene if maintenance levels are a concern.

10. Graph all data and utilize decision rules.

DISPLAYING DATA

For ease of analysis and communication with other educators, the school community, parents, and students, evaluation data need not be complicated. In addition, graphs do not have to be constructed or maintained by the adult supervising the intervention project. Students can use behavioral evaluations as an application of the basic mathematics skill of graphing. A disruptive student could earn the privilege of keeping a class graph for a period of time, or a responsible student can be assigned the task. Students whose behaviors have been targeted for remediation could display the evaluation data gathered on themselves.

Practical experience indicates that those who graph their own evaluation data make significantly better progress than those who do not (see the section in Chapter 4 on self-management). Although not terribly time-consuming, constructing and keeping graphs current can be one more unnecessary task for teachers and other school personnel. Therefore, whenever possible, students should construct and enter the data on the graphs.

Like many commonly used data displays, evaluation graphs consist of two axes, various labels, standard notations, some data calculations, and individual scores or plots. A checklist for constructing an evaluation graph is found in Table 5.2.

Raw data forms are helpful for creating a permanent record of the scores obtained each day the target behavior is measured. They provide a convenient way to organize this information. A different form is not necessary for each evaluation project. A standard form can be developed by a group of interested teachers, a committee appointed by the principal or counselor, or individual teachers. Generally, raw data may be organized in two ways, either on a form or on a graph (as in Figure 5.1). Table 5.3 shows a sample raw data form to be used as a permanent record of evaluation data. Raw data forms are particularly helpful when students graph data. If the daily scores are recorded in an organized fashion for a permanent file, the plots on the evaluation graph can be checked easily for accuracy.

The following points should be covered when explaining the graph to a student assigned to graph the evaluation data. There are two axes on

TABLE 5.2
Checklist for Constructing an Evaluation Graph

Task Completed	Step
	1. *Set up graph*
_____	Obtain standard graph paper
_____	Draw abscissa (horizontal line)
_____	Draw ordinate (vertical line)
_____	Label abscissa
_____	Label ordinate
_____	Indicate target behavior(s)
_____	Indicate student(s)' name(s)
_____	Indicate observation period
_____	Indicate teacher's name
_____	Date graph
_____	Indicate criterion or aim
	2. *Calculate data*
_____	Select measurement system
_____	Set up raw data sheet
_____	Calculate scores
	3. *Plot data*
_____	Place plot(s) on appropriate dayline
_____	Connect plots within phases
_____	Do not connect plots across student absences
_____	Connect plots across no-chance days
_____	Indicate phase changes with a solid vertical line
_____	Label phases
	4. *Analyze data*
_____	Calculate a mean or median for each phase
_____	Enter central tendency scores on graph for each phase

graphs. The *vertical axis*, or *ordinate*, is used for the measurement system. If duration is selected as the measurement system, the ordinate is so labeled. Hatch marks (–) should be placed along this axis, perhaps at points that correspond to multiples of five, so easy reference can be made as the data are plotted. The numbering system should allow enough room to plot all possible scores that could be obtained during each day or evaluation session. For example, if 100 pieces of litter could be picked up from the playground at the end of the day, the graph should allow for at least a score of 125. If an academic period of 40 minutes is used for the observation of a student's out-of-seat behavior, then 40 would be the highest score allowed on the ordinate.

TABLE 5.3
Sample Raw Data Sheet

Student's Name _____   Target Behavior _____

Teacher's Name _____   Standard Observation Time _____

Measurement System Used _____

Date	Day	Tally or no. of minutes	No. of opportunities or observation time	Percentage of occurrence	Comments
/ /	M				
	T				
	W				
	T				
	F				
/ /	M				
	T				
	W				
	T				
	F				
/ /	M				
	T				
	W				
	T				
	F				

The *horizontal axis*, or *abscissa*, is used for session days. Each vertical line on standard preprinted graph paper could represent a day of the school week or any other observation day. These are referred to as *daylines*. Even if the pupil is absent or school is not in session on a particular day of the week, the dayline always represents that day. In other words, Monday's dayline is Monday's dayline whether or not it is used. Thus, the abscissa could be labeled "Calendar Days," "School Days," or "Session Days." For educators who like to be able to see a week's set of data at a glance, "Calendar Days" is the best way to organize the abscissa; although daylines appear for Saturday and Sunday, they are always left blank, thereby demarking the school days. For educators who do not feel that including weekend days is helpful, the abscissa might be labeled "School Days." In this case, there are no daylines for Saturday and Sunday, and a continuous record of school days appears on the graph. Some teachers, such as a music teacher, see certain students fewer than five times a week. In such instances, the teacher might want to label the abscissa "Session Days" and thereby eliminate those days when observation cannot occur. (It is visually difficult to analyze data if only one or two plots appear per seven daylines.) Each educator must decide how to label the abscissa to fit the particular situation.

In addition to the axes labels, other information should be entered onto the graph. The name of the student, if an individual graph is kept, is important. Other pieces of information that many educators consider important are teacher's name, scheduled time of the day for observation, amount of observation time, the targeted behavior(s), and the date the project is initiated. Examples of where to enter this information can be found on the sample graph shown in Figure 5.1.

One other notation that many educators find helpful is the specification of the project's criterion, aim, or goal. Ruth is usually 10 minutes tardy each day she comes to history class. The teacher, Mr. Pepe, would like to see that time reduced to 1 minute. To indicate this goal to both himself and the student, he would enter an A (for "aim" score) on the vertical axis (the ordinate) at the desired score. This can serve as a reminder to both parties involved and clearly indicate the behavioral goal to the student.

Once the graph is set up, it can be used each day to enter the scores obtained by the end of the observation period. The data should be entered on the graphs immediately after they are collected and calculated, which allows for immediate feedback regarding performance and for quick and continual evaluation of student progress.

The plots or daily scores are entered on the graph so that they fall *on* the daylines and at the appropriate gradients as indicated on the vertical axis. For example, a score of 24 is plotted on the dayline representing the day on which it was collected, appropriately placed between the scores 20 and 25 as represented on the vertical axis.

Plots are usually entered on the graph as dots or small filled-in circles. When multiple sets of data are collected concurrently, different plotting notations can be used (e.g., Xs, filled-in triangles, open circles). This situation occurs when an educator wants to keep records of individual behaviors within a set. For example, a playground supervisor concerned about Jimmy's aggressive behavior at recess might keep separate records for hits, pushes, and threats. These could all be entered on the same graph with a different code for each behavior (e.g., a dot for hits, an X for pushes, and a triangle for threats).

Educators should follow standard conventions for connecting plots because they yield vital information that could affect project evaluation and intervention selection. Plots are connected within the phases. When a student is absent, that dayline is left blank and the plots around the absence are not connected. If data are lost or could not be collected due to scheduling difficulties at school, the dayline should be left blank. However, the plots preceding and following this *no-chance day* should be connected, allowing for a quick identification of one common cause of poor school work. If a student has an attendance problem, that must be addressed. Her entire academic schedule might need adjustment because she is unable to attend a particular class due to legitimate conflicts. This is important information, and it is easily noted by following the standard conventions for connecting plots.

If the horizontal axis is labeled "Calendar Days," Saturday and Sunday should be considered no-chance days. Therefore, Friday's plot is not connected to Monday's plot, allowing each week's worth of data to stand out distinctly. However, when "School Days" are used, Friday's and Monday's plots are connected to each other.

Whenever a change in phases occurs, a vertical line should be placed between the daylines that represent the last day of one phase and the first day of the next (see Figure 5.1). Plots are not connected across phase-change lines, so that data from the assessment phase are clearly distinguishable from the intervention phase, data from the intervention phase are separated from the maintenance phase, and the follow-up are clustered as another data unit. This separation of data gathered under different conditions allows for easier visual analysis of the data gathered during the project.

To assist in quick visual analysis, each phase should be clearly labeled, as in Figure 5.1. These labels usually appear across the top of the graph. The assessment phase should be labeled "Assessment," and each intervention phase should be labeled with a term describing the intervention implemented (e.g., "Praise," "Interdependent Group Contingency," "Restitutional Overcorrection"). These terms may be taken from the Intervention Ladder. The importance of labeling each phase precisely and concisely cannot be overemphasized. Labels are vital for communication and for future reference to know what the effects of various interventions were. If one tactic never proves effective, other educators might decide not to use it in future projects. Parents also should know what procedures employed at school produced desired results.

Some analysis of the data facilitates communication. Complicated formulas for analyzing the data gathered are not necessary for evaluating the effectiveness of interventions and for monitoring student progress. Simply calculating a central tendency score for each phase of a project is sufficient.

A central tendency score can be calculated using the mean, median, or mode. A mean is merely an average of the scores obtained for a phase. The daily or session scores are added together, then divided by the total number of scores. By using a hand-held calculator, most students can calculate mean scores without much difficulty. The median is the middle score by rank order, not temporal sequence. To obtain a median, one needs to know how to rank scores from highest to lowest and count. With a bit of practice, this becomes a very easy way to calculate a central tendency score. Figure 5.2 provides several examples of ways to determine median scores.

Only the mean and median are appropriate for behavioral evaluations, because it is not important to know which score was the most popular or frequent (the mode). What is important is to identify the score that best represents the scores obtained for each phase. Using a common score when discussing the success of a behavioral project is very useful. Rather than talking about each individual score, the educator can discuss the general performance level during each phase. This allows for a simple, quick discussion of progress made over time. Without a central tendency score for each phase, such condensed yet meaningful communication is impaired. For example, by having calculated a central tendency score for each phase,

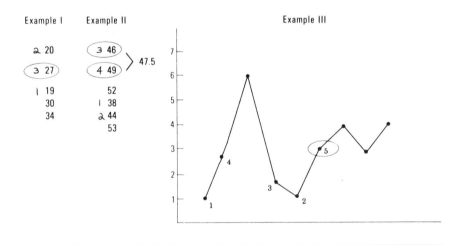

FIGURE 5.2. Calculating medians. Example I has five scores; the third score (27) is the median. Example II has six scores; the median (47.5) is halfway between scores 3 and 4. Example III has nine scores; the fifth score (3) is the median. From *Teaching Students with Learning and Behavior Problems* (2nd ed., p. 73) by D. D. Smith, 1989, Englewood Cliffs, NJ: Prentice-Hall. Copyright 1989 by Prentice-Hall. Reprinted with permission.

Mr. Patton was better able to communicate the progress Ladelle had made over 4 school weeks. During the assessment phase, Ladelle spent 35% of the school day complaining about school work or physical ailments. When an ignoring intervention was implemented, her complaining dropped to 5% and remained at that level during maintenance and follow-up.

The central tendency score for each phase is entered on the graph. If the mean is chosen to represent the central tendency score, it should be used throughout the project. If the median is selected, it should be used to represent each phase. Whichever method for calculating the central tendency is used, that score is entered in a circle within each phase section on the graph, as in Figure 5.1.

PRACTICE WHAT YOU'VE LEARNED

1. Define target behaviors that are observable and measurable that would be appropriate for a behavior change project. Provide nonexamples of target behaviors, that is, behaviors that do not meet the definition of observable and measurable (e.g., lazy, hyperactive).

2. Describe ways to identify target behaviors. The purpose is to identify precisely what behaviors are problematic.

3. Explain the measurement systems described in this chapter for recording occurrences of target behaviors. Provide examples of target behaviors that are most appropriately measured by the various measurement systems.

4. Design a behavior change plan, beginning with identifying the target behavior, collecting baseline, implementing an intervention that matches the infraction, and monitoring student progress using one or more measurement systems from this chapter.

5. Implement the behavior change plan described in item 4.

6. Chart the data from the behavior change plan, and describe the decision rules used to evaluate the plan's effectiveness. Brainstorm possible intervention alternatives if a change is necessary.

7. Brainstorm ways to implement behavior change plans, including collecting data while teaching.

8. Describe ways students and educational assistants can be used to collect data.

SUMMARY

The following are the important ideas discussed in this chapter.

1. The purposes of collecting evaluation data on student performance are to (a) obtain a record of the disturbance, (b) evaluate the effectiveness of the intervention selected, and (c) determine whether short- and long-term maintenance of those effects is sufficient once the criterion is met.

2. Systematically collecting information about a student's infractions allows the educator to check whether the target behavior is actually identified and whether it is serious enough to warrant intervention.

3. After the intervention is implemented, these data allow for an immediate evaluation of the effectiveness of the procedure selected. Modification of the remediation plan can be scheduled within a reasonable amount of time.

4. Once the goal or criterion is met, continued evaluation indicates whether performance gains are maintained at desired levels. If not, intervention should be reinstated. Without this sensitive and simple evaluation, educators do not know whether their educational planning produces successful outcomes.

5. By graphing the data collected, educators can quickly see the product of their educational planning and evaluation. Such graphs serve as a transcript of the behavioral occurrences throughout the project period.

6. Because of the conciseness and simplicity of the graphs, changes in student performance are readily communicated to parents, students, other educators, and the entire school community.

CHAPTER DISCUSSION QUESTIONS

1. What are examples of behaviors that can be measured?

2. How can behaviors be measured?

3. When should behaviors be measured?

4. Who should conduct the measurement?

5. What are examples of measurement systems?

6. What are the evaluation phases?

7. How can data be recorded?

6
Review

We designed this chapter to reinforce the concepts presented in this book. The chapter comprises review activities that give the reader an opportunity to apply the material covered throughout the text. We hope that the activities will stimulate thought about the prevention of conduct problems, the remediation of those problems through direct intervention, and the evaluation of intervention programs. Through these activities, the reader is encouraged to apply the book's content to real situations.

The review activities were designed for use by individuals or groups. An individual reader should be able to review the material by completing the activities and rereading the relevant sections of the text. Educators who are working together to find better ways to achieve discipline in their school settings can complete the activities, then discuss their ideas in group meetings. Regardless of the mode adopted for learning more about disciplinary techniques, the review sessions may be used in several ways. The entire book can be read before the review is begun, or individual chapters can be reviewed as they are read, using the corresponding review sessions. Those who are working together as a group or class might find it more efficient to do the activities as "homework" and use group time for discussion.

SESSION 1: LAYING THE FOUNDATION (CHAPTER 1)

Establishing a positive learning environment is critical to the goal of encouraging each student to achieve his or her potential. Discipline is part of this environment and must be integrated into the total educational experience. Educators must be cognizant of their philosophy about discipline and ways in which all individuals in the school community can work collaboratively to achieve a positive climate in which successful learning can occur. The following activities are intended to provoke thought and discussion about the need for discipline and its relationship to the educational atmosphere.

    A. Answer the following questions.

        1. What does discipline mean?

2. How do societal issues affect education?

3. What is your philosophy of education?

4. How is a schoolwide philosophy of education and discipline established?

5. What is your philosophy of discipline?

6. What are the primary goals of the educational system?

7. Would the public residing in your local community agree that discipline is a major concern of all individuals in the school community? Why or why not?

8. Why is it important for school personnel to work as a team to create a disciplinary plan?

9. How is a positive school climate fostered?

10. What are examples of disciplinary concerns shared by educators?

B. Indicate whether the following statements are true or false. Provide reasons for your answers.

_____ 1. The match between interventions and infractions of the code of conduct needs to be sensitive.

_____ 2. It is unrealistic to involve all members in the school community in establishing a code of conduct.

_____ 3. Discipline can result in social learning.

_____ 4. There are many ways to promote a sense of community among all individuals involved in educating students.

_____ 5. The reasons for discipline problems in school settings are insurmountable.

_____ 6. Violations of school norms of behavior are widespread, and the number of students requiring direct intervention for those violations is large.

_____ 7. There are many obstacles in establishing effective communication with parents and colleagues.

_____ 8. The establishment of a positive learning environment requires the use of elaborate and expensive procedures.

_____ 9. Discipline results in a repressive learning environment.

_____ 10. Maintaining consistency is easier said than done.

C. Explain the rationale and conceptual framework for the Intervention Ladder.

D. Provide several reasons why discipline can result in social learning for _all_ students.

E. Describe ways to establish a positive school climate.

F. Explain ways to involve faculty, staff, and parents in the school community.

G. Describe ways teachers can exert their influence in the classroom to establish a positive climate.

H. List examples of communication techniques when working with administrators, colleagues, and parents.

I. Describe how effective communication can be established in the classroom between the teacher and paraprofessional so consistency in disciplinary intervention is maintained.

J. Develop a list of guiding principles to remember when establishing a positive disciplinary climate.

SESSION 2: PREVENTING DISCIPLINARY PROBLEMS (CHAPTER 2)

The frequency of conduct problems that disrupt the learning environment can be reduced through the systematic use of various preventive measures. The activities and exercises below are designed to stimulate thought about the creation of a positive learning environment and about subtle ways to foster this climate.

A. Indicate whether the following statements are true or false. Identify the reasons for your answers.

_____ 1. Discipline is a major problem facing me at my school.

_____ 2. Discipline is something that educators can change.

_____ 3. Curriculum, instruction, and discipline are related.

_____ 4. All deportment problems must be met with direct intervention.

_____ 5. What is a discipline problem for one teacher may not be a problem for another.

_____ 6. The difficulties students have with discipline depend on the teacher and location.

_____ 7. Learning requires the extensive use of drill and practice.

_____ 8. There are too many extracurricular activities at my school.

_____ 9. More basic academic subjects should be required of every student.

_____ 10. Teachers should not have to adjust their instructional methods to compete with the world outside of school.

_____ 11. Every student who enters a school contest should be a winner.

_____ 12. Students and teachers should establish classroom expectations jointly.

_____ 13. Students who have discipline problems should be referred to special education.

_____ 14. Discipline and instructional procedures are unrelated.

_____ 15. Academic productivity and disruption are related.

_____ 16. A standard plan for discipline should be adopted at my school.

_____ 17. Educators should expect all students to respect their authority and thereby follow school codes of behavior.

_____ 18. All behavior problems occur consistently throughout the school day.

_____ 19. Transitional times must be managed as part of the instructional program.

B. Identify three specific prevention techniques that could be used in a classroom and three others that could be used schoolwide.

C. Describe practices that teachers can use to promote a preventive climate.

D. Rethink your schedule of activities for an academic period or entire school day. Develop a new schedule.

E. Explain why behavior problems occur.

F. List ways to prevent boredom and frustration.

G. List four ways to alter the instructional format to seek more active involvement and interest from students.

H. Discuss ways to motivate students.

I. Describe techniques that help students match appropriate behavioral responses with their environment.

J. List your classroom expectations. Add or delete new expectations to foster a positive climate.

K. Develop a plan to teach students how to transition appropriately.

L. Explain techniques that can enhance student academic success.

M. Indicate the level of disciplinary involvement appropriate for each of the following groups or individuals. Place one or more of the following letters in the blanks provided: T for total involvement, E for establishment of a code of conduct, S for selection of the disciplinary measures to be used, I for implementation of the disciplinary measures, and C for inclusion in a communication network.

_____ Students

_____ Teachers

_____ Speech–language pathologists

_____ Parents

_____ Custodians

_____ Coaches

_____ Paraprofessionals

_____ Administrators

_____ Counselors

_____ School secretary

_____ Nurse

_____ Bus drivers

N. Explain the importance of the environment in preventing discipline problems.

O. Brainstorm techniques for introducing subject content in novel and exciting ways.

P. Sketch a classroom layout that includes environmental considerations to prevent discipline problems.

SESSION 3: THE INTERVENTION LADDER, PART 1 (CHAPTER 3)

Despite actions taken by educators to prevent conduct problems, many problems persist. Direct intervention tactics are necessary to maintain a positive atmosphere in which learning can take place. Many times the interventions required are minimal, whereas at other times more intrusive tactics are necessary. It is important for educators to know about a wide variety of interventions. The activities presented in this and the next two review sessions aim to remind educators of the vast number of interventions available. Those with the highest probability of success should be scheduled first.

A. Review Table 3.3, the glossary for the Intervention Ladder, Part 1. Create your own examples for each tactic included in that glossary. Try to select examples that relate to your role in your school setting.

B. Discuss the precautions to consider for each of the following interventions:

1. Dependent, independent, and interdependent group contingencies

2. Ignoring

3. Contingent instructions

4. Fines

5. Rules

C. Indicate two pairs of disciplinary tactics that, when used together, produce better results. Provide examples of behaviors for which these pairs of tactics are most appropriate.

D. Design a criterion-specific rewards system. Explain how this system will be taught to students.

E. List your rules. Add or delete rules to enhance more effective discipline in your classroom. Write a lesson plan for how rules will be developed and explained. Include consequences for following and breaking the rules. Describe how your rules will be communicated to the administration and students' parents.

F. Discuss the rationale for using or not using each of the following tactics:

1. Criterion-specific rewards

2. Specific praise

3. Contingent observation

4. Group contingencies

5. Fines

6. Ignoring

G. Provide tips for implementing each of the following interventions:

1. Ignoring

2. Contingent observation

3. Rules

4. Group contingencies

SESSION 4: THE INTERVENTION LADDER, PART 2 (CHAPTER 4)

Although the preventive measures discussed in Chapters 1 and 2 and the milder interventions explained in Chapter 3 are sufficiently powerful to produce desired performance changes for the large majority of students, more drastic procedures are required for some students and specific situations. Rarely should the tactics presented in Part 2 be the first interventions selected. The activities in this session cover those interventions that are more intrusive or difficult to manage.

A. Review Table 4.2, the glossary for the Intervention Ladder, Part 2. Create your own examples for each tactic included in that glossary. Try to select examples that relate to your role in your school setting.

B. If you were the administrator, describe interventions you would use for the following behaviors. Explain your rationale.

1. Stealing

2. Carrying weapons on school property

3. Selling drugs on school property

4. Vandalizing school property

5. Writing on the bathroom walls

6. Smoking in the restrooms

7. Cutting classes

C. List precautions to consider for each of the following interventions:

1. Tutoring

2. In-school suspension

3. Suspension

4. Expulsion

5. Environmental restructuring

6. Self-management

7. Seclusion timeout

8. Punishment

9. Law enforcement agencies

10. Positive practice

D. Develop guidelines for use with each of the following procedures. List those behavioral infractions that match each.

1. Seclusion timeout

2. Restitution

3. Punishment

4. Suspension

5. Expulsion

E. Write a proposal (including rationale, objectives, staffing requirements, and space obligations) for the implementation of in-school supervision.

F. Describe important considerations for establishing a timeout room. Explain when timeout is appropriate and how this intervention is explained to parents.

G. Design an interdependent group contingency program. Describe the behavior(s) for which it will be used, the objectives, and implementation procedures.

SESSION 5: SELECTING AND APPLYING INTERVENTIONS (CHAPTERS 3 AND 4)

It is important for educators to know about a vast array of intervention techniques so that they can reduce or eliminate disruption quickly with the least intrusive intervention. Educators must know not only which intervention to apply in a specific situation, but also how to apply that intervention correctly. The activities designed for this session aim at strengthening knowledge about the selection and application of intervention tactics.

A. Analyze each of the following behavioral examples. Determine whether the best intervention was selected and applied. If not, suggest an intervention that would have been more likely to produce the desired results.

1. Brian was tardy to biology class one day. Mr. Taylor decided to implement a criterion-specific reward system for Brian.

2. Jeff talked back to his teachers. He refused to comply with the school rules regarding smoking in the corridors, making rude comments about the teachers, and using foul language. The teachers and administrators decided to expel him from school.

3. Debby wandered around the classroom too much. She did not spend enough time on task. Ms. Collins scheduled a dependent group contingency for Debby's improved academic production.

4. Ron was the class clown. He disturbed his classmates by telling jokes, making strange sounds, and contorting his face. Ms. Caldwell ignored him.

5. Diane complained frequently of a stomachache or not feeling well. She made many trips each day to the school nurse. Mr. Bryant sent Diane to seclusion timeout each time she claimed to be sick.

6. Larry fought on the playground at recess. Almost every day he picked on a smaller child and instigated a fight. Ms. Smiley decided to fine him for each occurrence of the behavior.

7. Lydia always left a mess in the cafeteria. She left the table dirty and never properly disposed of her litter. Mr. Lee selected environmental restructuring to stop the inappropriate behavior.

8. An inordinate amount of graffiti was drawn on the school walls. Mr. Smith, the principal, scheduled a specific praise intervention.

B. Develop examples of the inappropriate selection and application of two tactics found on the Intervention Ladder.

C. Develop a lesson plan for a training session in which students learn how to use one of the following tactics:

1. Peer behavioral management

2. Ignoring

3. Environmental restructuring

4. Rules

5. Dependent group contingency

6. Self-regulation

7. Self-evaluation

8. Self-reinforcement

9. Independent group contingency

10. Peer tutoring

D. Role play the actualization of the lesson plan prepared in the above activity.

E. Describe discipline concerns at your school and identify appropriate interventions from the Intervention Ladder.

SESSION 6: IDENTIFYING THE TARGET BEHAVIOR (CHAPTER 5)

Correctly identifying those behaviors that need remediation is one key to the success of every intervention program. A careful analysis of target behavior(s) should be completed before interventions are implemented. This will increase the likelihood of promoting the desired changes in student performance. The purpose of the activities below is to further sharpen those identification skills.

A. Provide four reasons why behaviors need to be specified carefully and completely before intervention plans are enacted.

B. List the steps to be followed when initially analyzing target behaviors.

C. Indicate, by writing "yes" or "no" in the space provided, whether the following behaviors are identified specifically enough for remediation efforts to begin. Provide a reason for your answer.

	Behavior	*Comments*
_____	Sullenness	_____
_____	Tardiness	_____
_____	Out-of-seat	_____
_____	Aggression	_____
_____	Defacing school property	_____
_____	Stealing	_____
_____	Littering	_____
_____	Talking out	_____
_____	Being too noisy	_____
_____	Exhibiting hyperactivity	_____
_____	Being lazy	_____
_____	Cussing	_____
_____	Interrupting teacher	_____

D. Provide reasons why many educators choose to remediate specific behaviors rather than underlying psychological constructs.

E. Indicate how educators should determine when (during what time period) a behavior should be measured.

F. Explain ways to identify the target behavior.

G. Provide examples of target behaviors that need to be remediated in your school and classroom.

SESSION 7: EVALUATING INTERVENTION PROGRAMS (CHAPTER 5)

Educators must know whether the procedures they have scheduled are producing the desired results. This information should be gathered while the intervention program is in effect. In this way, decisions can be made about terminating an intervention program because criteria were met, selecting another intervention tactic because sufficient changes were not noted, or retaining the intervention scheduled because progress is being made. Educators must be able to justify the intervention program to others (e.g., why the program was initiated, why the selected intervention tactic was selected, how effective the intervention was, and whether the program was successful). Sessions 7 and 8 review data collection systems and evaluation techniques. They should help the reader to integrate evaluations of student progress and program effectiveness and to refine abilities to evaluate student performance.

A. Using the data provided in Figure 6.1, complete the graph using the checklist provided in Table 5.2.

B. For the following behaviors, indicate whether frequency or duration data should be kept.

_____ Out-of-seat

_____ Littering

_____ Absences

_____ Tantrums

_____ Beginning an assignment when instructed to do so

_____ Late homework assignments

_____ Tardiness

_____ Interrupting teacher

_____ Completed assignments

_____ Swearing

NINE-WEEK CHART

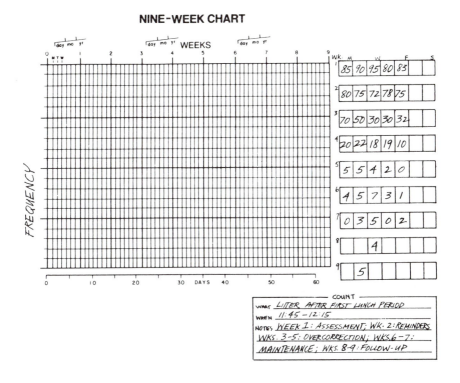

FIGURE 6.1. Evaluation graph to be completed. (See p. 217 for blackline master)

_____ Defaced library books

_____ Food fights

_____ Talking out of turn

C. List the four basic phases of every evaluation plan.

1. _____

2. _____

3. _____

4. _____

D. When should frequency and duration data be refigured to yield percentage scores?

E. Construct lesson plans to teach students how to graph evaluation data.

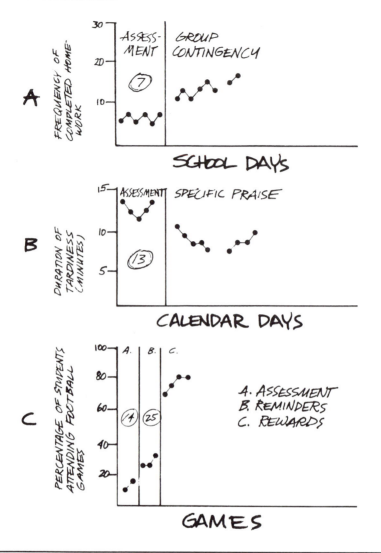

FIGURE 6.2. Graphs for making decisions about future interventions.

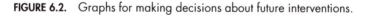

    F. Role play one lesson plan developed in the above activity.

    G. Describe ways to evaluate whether the intervention plan is working.

SESSION 8: MAKING DATA DECISIONS (CHAPTER 5)

Making decisions from data leads to more efficient educational programming. It takes some practice to make conclusions about the effectiveness of intervention programs from graphic displays of data. The activities included in this session should provide preliminary practice for making speedy yet accurate decisions about the results of scheduled interventions.

A. Give reasons why traditional pre- and posttesting methods (e.g., September and June evaluations) are not adequate for behavioral evaluations. Describe more appropriate time frames for evaluating student progress.

B. What are the limitations of the measurement systems described in this book?

C. Three partial evaluation graphs are shown in Figure 6.2. Study each graph and indicate what you would do next for each situation displayed.

D. When should an intervention plan be terminated and a new plan implemented?

E. Develop an outline for a parent conference designed to share the results from an evaluation of a behavioral project.

F. Develop an outline for sharing the results from an evaluation of a behavioral project at a staffing meeting.

G. Define a target behavior. Identify an appropriate intervention match. Select an evaluation system. Implement the intervention. Collect data. Make decisions regarding student progress.

References

Alberto, P. A., & Troutman, A. C. (1990). *Applied behavior analysis for teachers* (3rd ed.). New York: Macmillan.

Allen, K. E., Hart, B. M., Buell, J. S., Harris, F. R., & Wolf, M. M. (1964). Effects of social reinforcement on isolate behavior of a nursery school child. *Child Development, 35*, 511–518.

Axelrod, S., & Apsche, J. (Eds.). (1983). *The effects of punishment on human behavior.* New York: Academic Press.

Axelrod, S., Brantner, J. P., & Meddock, T. D. (1978). Overcorrection: A review and critical analysis. *The Journal of Special Education, 12*, 367–391.

Ayllon, T., Garber, S., & Pisor, K. (1975). The elimination of discipline problems through a combined school–home motivational system. *Behavior Therapy, 6*, 616–626.

Ayllon, T., & Roberts, M. D. (1974). Eliminating discipline problems by strengthening academic performance. *Journal of Applied Behavior Analysis, 7*, 71–76.

Azrin, N. H., & Powers, M. A. (1975). Eliminating classroom disturbances of emotionally disturbed children by positive practice procedures. *Behavior Therapy, 6*, 525–534.

Bacon, E. H. (1990). Using negative consequences effectively. *Academic Therapy, 25*, 599–611.

Baron, R. A. (1988). Negative effects of destructive criticism: Impact on conflict, self-efficacy, and task performance. *Journal of Applied Psychology, 73*, 199–207.

Barrish, H. H., Saunders, M., & Wolf, M. M. (1969). Good behavior game: Effects of individual contingencies for group consequence on disruptive behavior in a classroom. *Journal of Applied Behavior Analysis, 2*, 119–124.

Bartlett, L. (1989). Disciplining handicapped students: Legal issues in light of Honig v. Doe. *Exceptional Children, 55*, 357–366.

Bickell, W. E., & Bickell, D. D. (1986). Effective schools, classrooms, and instruction: Implications for special education. *Exceptional Children, 52*, 489–500.

Billingsley, F. F. (1977). The effects of self- and externally-imposed schedules of reinforcement on oral reading performance. *Journal of Learning Disabilities, 10*, 549–559.

Broden, M., Hall, R. V., Dunlap, A., & Clark, R. (1970). Effects of teacher attention and a token reinforcement system in a junior high school special education class. *Exceptional Children, 36*, 341–349.

Broden, M., Hall, R. V., & Mitts, B. (1971). The effect of self-recording on the classroom behavior of two eighth-grade students. *Journal of Applied Behavior Analysis, 4*, 191–199.

Buckley, N. K., & Walker, H. M. (1978). *Modifying classroom behavior: A manual of procedures for classroom teachers* (revised ed.). Champaign, IL: Research Press.

Burke, J. C. (1992). *Decreasing classroom behavior problems.* San Diego: Singular Publishing Group.

Canter, L. (1986). *Assertive discipline: A take-charge approach for today's educator.* Los Angeles: Canter and Associates.

Carey, R. J., & Bucher, B. (1983). Positive practice overcorrection: The effects of duration of positive practice on acquisition and response reduction. *Journal of Applied Behavior Analysis, 16,* 101–109.

Center, D. B., Deitz, S. M., & Kaufman, M. E. (1982). Student ability, task difficulty, and inappropriate classroom behavior: A study of children with behavior disorders. *Behavior Modification, 6,* 355–374.

Charles, C. M. (1981). *Building classroom discipline: From models to practice.* New York: Longman.

Chiang, B., Thorpe, H. W., & Darch, C. B. (1980). Effects of cross-age tutoring on word-recognition performance of learning disabled students. *Learning Disability Quarterly, 3,* 11–19.

Clarizio, H. F. (1980). *Toward positive classroom discipline* (3rd ed.). New York: Wiley.

Cone, J. P., DeLawyer, D. D., & Wolfe, V. V. (1985). Assessing parent participation: The parent/family involvement index. *Exceptional Children, 51,* 417–424.

Cooper, J. O., & Edge, D. (1978). *Parenting strategies and educational methods.* Columbus, OH: Merrill.

Cowen, R. J., Jones, F. H., & Bellack, A. S. (1979). Grandma's rule with group contingencies—A cost-efficient means of classroom management. *Behavior Modification, 3,* 397–418.

Devin-Sheehan, L., Feldman, R. S., & Allen, V. L. (1976). Research on children tutoring children: A critical review. *Review of Educational Research, 46,* 355–385.

Dickerson, E. A., & Creedon, C. F. (1981). Self-selection of standards by children: The relative effectiveness of pupil-selected and teacher-selected standards of performance. *Journal of Applied Behavior Analysis, 14,* 425–433.

Dietz, D. E. D., & Repp, A. C. (1983). Reducing behavior through reinforcement. *Exceptional Education Quarterly, 3,* 34–36.

Deitz, S. M., & Repp, A. C. (1973). Decreasing classroom misbehavior through the use of the DRL schedules of reinforcement. *Journal of Applied Behavior Analysis, 6,* 457–463.

Dreikurs, R., & Grey, L. (1970). *A parents' guide to child discipline.* New York: Hawthorne Books.

Ellis, E. S. (1986). The role of motivation and pedagogy on the generalization of cognitive strategy training. *Journal of Learning Disabilities, 19,* 66–70.

Ellis, E. S., & Friend, P. (1991). Adolescents with learning disabilities. In B. Y. L. Wong (Ed.), *Learning about learning disabilities* (pp. 505–561). San Diego: Academic Press.

Emmer, E. T., Evertson, C. M., Sanford, J. P., Clements, B. S., & Worsham, M. E. (1984). *Classroom management for secondary teachers*. Englewood Cliffs, NJ: Prentice-Hall.

Evertson, C. M., Emmer, E. T., Clements, B. S., Sanford, J. P., & Worsham, M. E. (1984). *Classroom management for elementary teachers*. Englewood Cliffs, NJ: Prentice-Hall.

Fagen, S. A., & Long, N. J. (1976). Teaching children self-control: A new responsibility for teachers. *Focus on Exceptional Children, 7*, 1–10.

Fagen, S. A., Long, N. J., & Stevens, D. J. (1975). *Teaching children self-control. Preventing emotional and learning problems in the elementary school*. Columbus, OH: Merrill.

Fantuzzo, J. W., & Clement, P. W. (1981). Generalization of the effects of teacher and self-administered token reinforcers to nontreated students. *Journal of Applied Behavior Analysis, 14*, 435–447.

Felixbrod, J. J., & O'Leary, K. D. (1973). Effects of reinforcement on children's academic behavior as a function of self-determined and externally imposed exigencies. *Journal of Applied Behavior Analysis, 6*, 241–250.

Ferritor, D. E., Buckholdt, D., Hamblin, R. L., & Smith, L. (1972). The non-effects of contingent reinforcement for attending behavior on work accomplished. *Journal of Applied Behavior Analysis, 5*, 7–17.

Fishbein, J. E., & Wasik, B. H. (1981). Effect of the good behavior game on disruptive library behavior. *Journal of Applied Behavior Analysis, 14*, 89–94.

Foxx, R. M. (1982). *Decreasing behavior of severely retarded and autistic persons*. Champaign, IL: Research Press.

Foxx, R. M., & Azrin, N. H. (1972). Restitution: A method of eliminating aggressive–disruptive behavior of retarded and brain-damaged patients. *Behavior Research and Therapy, 10*, 15–27.

Foxx, R. M., & Bechtel, D. R. (1983). Overcorrection: A review and analysis. In S. Axelrod & J. P. Apsche (Eds.), *The effects of punishment on human behavior* (pp. 133–220). New York: Academic Press.

Gallup, A. M. (1984). The Gallup poll of teachers' attitudes toward the public schools. *Phi Delta Kappan, 67*, 43–59.

Gallup, A. M. (1986). The 16th Gallup poll on the public's attitudes toward the public schools. *Phi Delta Kappan, 67*, 43–59.

Gast, D. L., & Nelson, C. M. (1977a). Legal and ethical considerations for the use of timeout in special education settings. *The Journal of Special Education, 11*, 457–467.

Gast, D., & Nelson, C. M. (1977b). Time out in the classroom: Implications for special education. *Exceptional Children, 43*, 461–464.

Glynn, E. L. (1970). Classroom applications of self-determined reinforcement. *Journal of Applied Behavior Analysis, 3*, 123–132.

Gordon, T. (1974). *Parent effectiveness training*. New York: A Plume Book, Times Mirror.

Goss v. Lopez. (1975). 419 U.S. 565 (U.S. Supreme Court).

Gresham, F. M., & Gresham, G. N. (1982). Interdependent, dependent, and independent group contingencies for controlling disruptive behavior. *The Journal of Special Education, 16,* 101–110.

Haisley, F. B., Tell, C. A., & Andrews, J. (1981). Peers as tutors in the mainstream: Trained "teachers" of handicapped adolescents. *Journal of Learning Disabilities, 14,* 224–226.

Hall, R. V., & Hall, M. C. (1980). *How to select reinforcers.* Austin: PRO-ED.

Hallahan, D. P., Hall, R. J., Ianna, S. O., Kneedler, R. D., Lloyd, J. W., Loper, A. B., & Reeve, R. E. (1983). Summary of research findings at the University of Virginia Learning Disabilities Research Institute. *Exceptional Education Quarterly, 4,* 95–113.

Hallahan, D. P., Lloyd, J., Kosiewicz, M. M., Kauffman, J. M., & Graves, A. W. (1979). Self-monitoring of attention as a treatment for a learning disabled boy's off-task behavior. *Learning Disability Quarterly, 2,* 24–32.

Hallahan, D. P., Marshall, K. J., & Lloyd, J. W. (1981). Self-recording during group instruction: Effects on attention to task. *Learning Disability Quarterly, 4,* 407–413.

Hallenback, M., & Beernick, M. (1989). A support program for parents of students with mild handicaps. *Teaching Exceptional Children, 21*(3), 44–47.

Harris, K. R. (1986). Self-monitoring of attentional behavior versus self-monitoring of productivity—Effects on on-task behavior and academic response rate among learning disabled children. *Journal of Applied Behavior Analysis, 19,* 417–423.

Heron, T. E. (1978). Punishment: A review of the literature with implications for the teacher of mainstreamed children. *The Journal of Special Education, 12,* 243–252.

Hewett, F. M. (1980). *The emotionally disturbed child in the classroom* (3rd ed.). Boston: Allyn & Bacon.

Hobbs, N. (1975). *The futures of children.* San Francisco: Jossey-Bass.

Hughes, C. A., & Boyle, J. R. (1991). Effects of self-monitoring for on-task behavior and task productivity on elementary students with moderate mental retardation. *Education and Treatment of Children, 14,* 96–111.

Ingraham v. Wright. (1977). 430 U.S. 651 (U.S. Supreme Court).

Jenkins, J. R., & Jenkins, L. M. (1981). *Cross age help for children with learning problems.* Reston, VA: Council for Exceptional Children.

Kneedler, R. D., & Hallahan, D. P. (1981). Self-monitoring of on-task behavior with learning disabled children: Current studies and directions. *Exceptional Education Quarterly, 2,* 73–82.

Kounin, J. S. (1970). *Discipline and group management in classrooms.* New York: Holt, Rhinehart & Winston.

Kramer, J. J. (1990). Best practices in parent training. In A. Thomas & J. Grimes (Eds.), *Best practices in school psychology–II* (pp. 263–273). Washington, DC: National Association of School Psychologists.

Kroth, R. L. (1985). *Communicating with parents of exceptional children: Improving parent-teacher relationships.* Denver: Love.

Kroth, R. L., & Simpson, R. L. (1977). *Parent conferences as a teaching strategy.* Denver: Love.

Krumboltz, J. D., & Krumboltz, H. B. (1972). *Changing children's behavior.* Englewood Cliffs, NJ: Prentice-Hall.

Kunzelmann, H. P., Cohen, M. A., Hutten, W. J., Martin, G. L., & Mingo, A. R. (1970). *Precision teaching: An initial training sequence.* Seattle: Special Child.

Lane, H. (1976). *The wild boy of Aveyron.* Cambridge: Harvard University Press.

Litow, L., & Pumroy, D. K. (1975). A brief review of classroom group-oriented contingencies. *Journal of Applied Behavior Analysis, 8,* 341–347.

Lloyd, J. W., Hallahan, D. P., Kosiewicz, M. M., & Kneedler, R. D. (1982). Reactive effects of self-assessment and self-recording on attention to task and academic productivity. *Learning Disabilities Quarterly, 6,* 216–227.

Long, J. D., & Frye, V. H. (1977). *Making it till Friday: A guide to successful classroom management.* Princeton, NJ: Princeton Book.

Lovitt, T. C. (1984). *Tactics for teaching.* Columbus, OH: Merrill.

Lovitt, T. C., & Curtiss, K. A. (1969). Academic response rate as a function of teacher- and self-imposed contingencies. *Journal of Applied Behavior Analysis, 2,* 49–53.

Lovitt, T. C., Lovitt, A. O., Eaton, M. D., & Kirkwood, M. (1973). The deceleration of inappropriate comments by a natural consequence. *Journal of School Psychology, 11,* 148–154.

Lovitt, T. C., & Smith, D. D. (1974). Using withdrawal of positive reinforcement to alter subtraction performance. *Exceptional Children, 40,* 357–358.

Lowe, J., & Smith, D. D. (1982). *Self-management techniques to improve middle school students' arithmetic proficiency.* Unpublished manuscript, Department of Special Education, University of New Mexico, Albuquerque.

Maheady, L., & Harper, G. (1987). A class-wide peer tutoring program to improve the spelling test performance of low-income, third- and fourth-grade students. *Educational Treatment of Children, 10,* 120–133.

Maurer, R. (1988). *Special education discipline handbook.* West Nyack, NY: Center for Applied Research in Education.

McKenzie, H. S., Clark, M., Wolf, M. M., Kothera, R., & Benson, C. (1968). Behavior modification of children with learning disabilities using grades as tokens and allowances as back up reinforcers. *Exceptional Children, 34,* 745–752.

Mercer, C. D. (1991). *Students with learning disabilities.* New York: Merrill.

Nelson, R. O., & Hayes, S. C. (1981). Theoretical explanations for reactivity in self-monitoring. *Behavior Modification, 5*(1), 3–14.

New Mexico State Department of Education. (1981). *Rights and responsibilities of public school students.* Santa Fe: Author.

O'Leary, K. D., Kaufman, D. F., Kass, R. E., & Drabman, R. S. (1970). The effects of loud and soft reprimands on the behavior of disruptive students. *Exceptional Children, 37,* 145–155.

O'Leary, K. D., & O'Leary, S. G. (1977). *Classroom management: The successful use of behavior modification* (2nd ed.). Elmsford, New York: Pergamon Press.

Poling, A., & Ryan, C. (1982). Differential-reinforcement-of-other-behavior schedules: Therapeutic applications. *Behavior Modification, 6,* 3–21.

Polsgrove, L., & Rieth, H. (1983). Procedures for reducing children's inappropriate behavior in special education settings. *Exceptional Education Quarterly, 3,* 20–33.

Premack, D. (1959). Toward empirical behavior laws: Positive reinforcement. *Psychological Review, 66,* 219–233.

Raschke, D., Stainback, S., & Stainback, W. (1982). The predictive capabilities of three sources for a promised consequence. *Behavior Disorders, 7*(4), 213–218.

Repp, A. C., & Deitz, D. E. (1978). On the selective use of punishment—Suggested guidelines for administrators. *Mental Retardation, 16,* 250–254.

Rieth, H. J., Polsgrove, L., & Semmel, M. I. (1981). Instructional variables that make a difference: Attention to task and beyond. *Exceptional Education Quarterly, 2,* 61–71.

Risley, T. R. (1968). The effects and side effects of punishing the autistic behaviors of a deviant child. *Journal of Applied Behavior Analysis, 1,* 21–34.

Rivera, D. M., & Smith, D. D. (1987). Influence of modeling on acquisition and generalization of computational skills: A summary of research findings from three sites. *Learning Disability Quarterly, 10,* 69–80.

Roberts, M. B., & Smith, D. D. (1977). The influence of contingent instructions on the social behavior of a young boy. *School Applications of Learning Theory, 9,* 24–42.

Robin, A., Schneider, M., & Dolnick, M. (1977). The turtle technique: An extended case study of self control in the classroom. In K. D. O'Leary & S. G. O'Leary (Eds.), *Classroom management. The successful use of behavior modification* (2nd ed.). New York: Pergamon Press.

Rose, T. L. (1988). Current disciplining practices with handicapped students: Suspensions and expulsions. *Exceptional Children, 55,* 230–239.

Rosenbaum, M. S., & Drabman, R. S. (1979). Self-control training in the classroom: A review and critique. *Journal of Applied Behavior Analysis, 12,* 467–485.

Rutherford, R. B., Jr., & Edgar, E. (1979). *Teachers and parents: A guide to interaction and cooperation.* Boston: Allyn & Bacon.

Sabatino, A. (1983). Prevention: Teachers' attitude and adaptive behavior—Suggested techniques. In D. A. Sabatino, A. C. Sabatino, & L. Mann, *Discipline and behavioral management* (pp. 29–84). Austin, TX: PRO-ED.

Salend, S. J. (1987). Group oriented behavior management strategies. *Teaching Exceptional Children, 20,* 53–55.

Salend, S. J., & Lamb, E. A. (1986). Effectiveness of a group-managed interdependent contingency system. *Journal of Learning Disabilities, 19,* 268–273.

Sapon-Shevin, M. (1982). Ethical issues in parent training programs. *The Journal of Special Education, 16,* 341–357.

Schloss, P. J. (1987). Self-management strategies for adolescents entering the work force. *Teaching Exceptional Children, 19*(4), 39–43.

Smith, D. D. (1989). *Teaching students with learning and behavior problems* (2nd ed.). Englewood Cliffs, NJ: Prentice-Hall.

Smith, J. D., Polloway, E. A., & West, G. K. (1979). Corporal punishment and its implications for exceptional children. *Exceptional Children, 45,* 264–269.

Strain, P. S. (1981). Peer-mediated treatment of exceptional children's social withdrawal. *Exceptional Education Quarterly, 1,* 93–105.

Sulzbacher, S. I., & Houser, J. E. (1968). A tactic to eliminate disruptive behaviors in the classroom: Group contingent consequences. *American Journal of Mental Deficiency, 73,* 88–90.

Thomas, J. W. (1980). Agency and achievement: Self-management and self-regard. *Review of Educational Research, 50,* 213–240.

Van Houten, R., Nau, P. A., McKenzie-Keating, D. E., Sameoto, D., & Colavecchia, B. (1982). An analysis of some variables influencing the effectiveness of reprimands. *Journal of Applied Behavior Analysis, 15,* 65–83.

Wagonseller, B. R., & McDowell, R. L. (1982). *Teaching involved parenting.* Champaign, IL: Research Press.

Walker, H. M. (1983). Applications of response cost in school settings: Outcomes, issues and recommendations. *Exceptional Educational Quarterly, 3,* 47–55.

White, G. D., Nielsen, G., & Johnson, S. M. (1972). Time-out duration and the suppression of deviant behavior in children. *Journal of Applied Behavior Analysis, 5,* 111–120.

White, M. A. (1975). Natural rates of teacher approval and disapproval in the classroom. *Journal of Applied Behavior Analysis, 8,* 367–372.

Windell, J. (1991). *Discipline: A source of 50 failsafe techniques for parents.* New York: Macmillan.

Wolf, J. S., & Stephens, T. M. (1990). Friends of special education: A parent training model. *Journal of Educational and Psychological Consultation, 1,* 343–356.

Wood v. Strickland. (1975). 420 U.S. 308 (U.S. Supreme Court).

Workman, E. A. (1982). *Teaching behavioral self-control to students.* Austin, TX: PRO-ED.

Yell, M. L. (1989). Honig v. Doe: The suspension of handicapped students. *Exceptional Children, 56,* 60–69.

APPENDIX

Suggested Readings

This reading list is organized according to the "rungs" of the Intervention Ladder presented in Figure 1.1, and is intended to direct the reader to sources of additional information on the various interventions. Included in the list are research articles that detail intervention techniques and results, reviews of the professional literature regarding the efficacy of certain interventions, and books that contain informative sections on the intervention under which they are listed. Additional readings are also suggested in the areas of behavioral evaluation, legal considerations involved in school discipline, and general material about discipline. A final section is devoted to school violence and crime.

FOUNDATION

Charles, C. M. (1981). *Building classroom discipline: From models to practice.* New York: Longman.

Cone, J. P., DeLawyer, D. D., & Wolfe, V. V. (1985). Assessing parent participation: The parent/family involvement index. *Exceptional Children, 51*, 417–424.

Ellis, E. S., & Friend, P. (1991). Adolescents with learning disabilities. In B. Y. L. Wong (Ed.), *Learning about learning disabilities* (pp. 505–561). San Diego: Academic Press.

Gallup, A. M. (1986). The 16th Gallup poll on the public's attitudes toward the public schools. *Phi Delta Kappan, 67*, 43–59.

Kounin, J. S. (1970). *Discipline and group management in classrooms.* New York: Holt, Rhinehart & Winston.

Madsen, C. H., & Madsen, C. K. (1981). *Teaching discipline* (3rd ed.). Boston: Allyn & Bacon.

Millman, H. L., Schaefer, C. E., & Cohen, J. J. (1977). *Therapies for school behavior problems.* San Francisco: Jossey-Bass.

Sabatino, A. (1983). Discipline: A national issue. In D. A. Sabatino, A. C. Sabatino, & L. Mann, *Discipline and behavioral management* (pp. 1–28). Austin, TX: PRO-ED.

PREVENTION

Ayllon, T., & Roberts, M. D. (1974). Eliminating discipline problems by strengthening academic performance. *Journal of Applied Behavior Analysis, 7*, 71–76.

Bickel, H. J., Polsgrove, L., & Semmel, M. I. (1981). Instructional variables that make a difference: Attention to task and beyond. *Exceptional Education Quarterly, 2,* 61–71.

Center, D. B., Deitz, S. M., & Kaufman, N. E. (1982). Student ability, task difficulty, and inappropriate classroom behavior: A study of children with behavioral disorders. *Behavior Modification, 6,* 355–374.

Charles, C. M. (1981). *Building classroom discipline: From models to practice.* New York: Longman.

Leithwood, K. A., & Montgomery, D. J. (1982). The role of the elementary school principal in program improvement. *Review of Educational Research, 52,* 309–339.

Lovitt, T. C. (1977). *In spite of my resistance, I've learned from children.* Columbus, OH: Merrill.

Lovitt, T. C. (1983). *Because of my persistence, I've learned from children.* Columbus, OH: Merrill.

Peterson, R. F., Loveless, S. E., Knapp, T. J., Loveless, B. W., Basta, S. M., & Anderson, S. (1979). The effects of teacher use of I-messages on student disruptive and study behavior. *Psychological Review, 29,* 187–199.

Rieth, H. J., & Bickel, D. D. (1986). Effective schools, classrooms, and instruction: Implications for special education. *Exceptional Children, 52,* 489–500.

SPECIFIC PRAISE

Kennedy, W. A., & Willcutt, H. C. (1964). Praise and blame as incentives. *Psychological Bulletin, 62,* 323–332.

Thomas, J. D., Presland, I. E., Grant, M. D., & Glynn, T. L. (1978). Natural rates of teacher approval and disapproval in grade 7 classrooms. *Journal of Applied Behavior Analysis, 11,* 91–94.

White, M. A. (1975). Natural rates of teacher approval and disapproval in the classroom. *Journal of Applied Behavior Analysis, 8,* 367–372.

IGNORING

O'Leary, K. D., & O'Leary, S. G. (1977). *Classroom management: The successful use of behavior modification.* New York: Plenum Press.

Sulzer-Azaroff, B., & Mayer, G. (1977). *Applying behavior analysis procedures with children and youth* (2nd ed.). New York: Holt, Rinehart & Winston.

RULES

Duke, D. L. (1980). *Managing student behavior problems.* New York: Columbia University Teachers College Press.

Long, J. D., & Frye, V. H. (1977). *Making it till Friday: A guide to successful classroom management.* Princeton, NJ: Princeton Book.

Lovitt, T. C. (1978). *Managing inappropriate behaviors in the classroom.* Reston, VA: Council for Exceptional Children.

CONTINGENT INSTRUCTIONS

O'Leary, K. D., Kaufman, K. F., Kass, R. E., & Drabman, R. S. (1970). The effects of loud and soft reprimands on the behavior of disruptive students. *Exceptional Children, 37,* 145–155.

Robert, M. B., & Smith, D. D. (1977). The influence of contingent instructions on the social behavior of a young boy. *School Applications of Learning Theory, 9,* 24–42.

CRITERION-SPECIFIC REWARDS

Axelrod, S. (1983). *Behavior modification for the classroom teacher* (2nd ed.). New York: McGraw-Hill.

Deitz, D. E. D., & Repp, A. C. (1983). Reducing behavior through reinforcement. *Exceptional Education Quarterly, 3,* 34–36.

Emmer, E. T., Evertson, C. M., Sanford, J. P., Clements, B. S., & Worsham, M. E. (1984). *Classroom management for secondary teachers.* Englewood Cliffs, NJ: Prentice-Hall.

Kazdin, A. E. (1977). *The token economy: A review and evaluation.* New York: Plenum Press.

FINES

Kazdin, A. E. (1977). *The token economy: A review and evaluation.* New York: Plenum Press.

Lovitt, T. C., & Smith, D. D. (1974). Using withdrawal of positive reinforcement to alter subtraction performance. *Exceptional Children, 40,* 357–358.

Martin, G., & Pear, J. (1978). *Behavior modification: What it is and how to do it.* Englewood Cliffs, NJ: Prentice-Hall.

O'Leary, S. G., & Dubey, D. R. (1979). Applications for self-control procedures by children: A review. *Journal of Applied Behavior Analysis, 1,* 449–465.

Rosenbaum, M. S., & Drabman, R. S. (1979). Self-control training in the classroom: A review and critique. *Journal of Applied Behavior Analysis, 12,* 467–485.

Walker, H. M. (1983). Applications of response cost in school settings: Outcomes, issues and recommendations. *Exceptional Education Quarterly, 3,* 47–55.

Workman, E. A. (1982). *Teaching behavioral self-control to students.* Austin, TX: PRO-ED.

GROUP CONTINGENCIES

Cowen, R. J., Jones, F. H., & Bellack, A. S. (1979). Grandma's rule with group contingencies—A cost-efficient means of classroom management. *Behavior Modification, 3,* 397–418.

Litow, L., & Pumroy, D. K. (1975). A brief review of classroom group-oriented contingencies. *Journal of Applied Behavior Analysis, 8*, 341–347.

PEER MANAGEMENT

Ehly, S., & Larsen, S. C. (1980). *Peer tutoring for individualized instruction.* Austin, TX: PRO-ED.

Jenkins, J. R., & Jenkins, L. M. (1981). *Cross age and peer tutoring: Help for children with learning problems.* Reston, VA: Council for Exceptional Children.

Krouse, J., Gerber, M. M., & Kaufmann, J. M. (1981). *Peer tutoring: Procedures, promises, and unresolved issues.* Rockville, MD: Aspen.

Strain, P. S. (1981). Peer-mediated treatment of exceptional children's social withdrawal. *Exceptional Education Quarterly, 1*, 93–105.

SELF-MANAGEMENT

Ellis, E. S. (1986). The role of motivation and pedagogy on the generalization of cognitive strategy training. *Journal of Learning Disabilities, 19*(2), 66–70.

Fagan, S. A., Long, N. J., & Stevens, D. J. (1975). *Teaching children self control: Preventing emotional and learning problems in the elementary school.* Columbus, OH: Merrill.

Karoly, P., & Kanfer, F. H. (Eds.). (1982). *Self management and behavior change: From theory to practice.* New York: Pergamon Press.

Kunzelmann, H. P., Cohen, M. A., Hutten, W. J., Martin, G. L., & Mingo, A. R. (1970). *Precision teaching: An initial training sequence.* Seattle: Special Child.

Lovitt, T. C. (1984). *Tactics for teaching* Columbus, OH: Merrill.

Meichenbaum, D. (1977). *Cognitive behavior modification: An integrative approach.* New York: Plenum Press.

O'Leary, S. G., & Dubey, D. R. (1979). Applications for self-control procedures by children: A review. *Journal of Applied Behavior Analysis, 12*, 449–465.

Rosenbaum, M. S., & Drabman, R. S. (1979). Self-control training in the classroom: A review and critique. *Journal of Applied Behavior Analysis, 12*, 467–485.

Workman, E. A. (1982). *Teaching behavioral self-control to students.* Austin, TX: PRO-ED.

PARENT INVOLVEMENT

Cooper, J. O., & Edge, D. (1978). *Parenting strategies and educational methods.* Columbus, OH: Merrill.

Kroth, R. L. (1985). *Communicating with parents of exceptional children: Improving parent–teacher relationships.* Denver: Love.

Kroth, R. L., & Simpson, R. L. (1977). *Parent conferences as a teaching strategy.* Denver: Love.

Losen, S. M., & Diament, B. (1978). *Parent conferences in the schools: Procedures for developing effective partnership.* Boston: Allyn & Bacon.

McDowell, R. L. (1978). *Managing behavior: A parent involvement program.* Torrance, CA: Winch Associates.

Rutherford, R. B., Jr., & Edgar, E. (1979). *Teachers and parents: A guide to interaction and cooperation.* Boston: Allyn & Bacon.

OVERCORRECTION

Axelrod, S., Brantner, J. P., & Meddock, T. D. (1978). Overcorrection: A review and critical analysis. *The Journal of Special Education, 12,* 367–391.

Carey, R. J., & Bucher, B. (1983). Positive practice overcorrection: The effects of duration of positive practice on acquisition and response reduction. *Journal of Applied Behavior Analysis, 16*(1), 101–109.

Foxx, R. M., & Bechtel, D. R. (1983). Overcorrection: A review and analysis. In S. Axelrod & J. P. Apsche (Eds.), *The effects of punishment on human behavior* (pp. 133–220). New York: Academic Press.

Marholin, D., II, Luiselli, J. K., & Townsend, N. M. (1980). Overcorrection: An examination of its rationale and treatment effectiveness. In M. Hersen, R. M. Eisler, & P. M. Miller (Eds.), *Progress in behavior modification* (Vol. 9). New York: Academic Press.

TIME OUT

Bacon, E. H. (1990). Using negative consequences effectively. *Academic Therapy, 25,* 599–611.

Bacon, R. A. (1988). Negative effects of destructive criticism: Impact on conflict, self-efficacy, and task performance. *Journal of Applied Psychology, 73,* 199–207.

Foxx, R. M. (1982). *Decreasing behavior of severely retarded and autistic persons.* Champaign, IL: Research Press.

Gast, D. L., & Nelson, C. M. (1977). Legal and ethical considerations for the use of timeout in special education settings. *Journal of Special Education, 11,* 457–467.

Nelson, M. C., & Rutherford, R. B. (1983). Timeout revisited: Guidelines for its use in special education. *Exceptional Education Quarterly, 3,* 56–67.

Sulzer-Azaroff, B., & Mayer, G. (1977). *Applying behavior analysis procedures with children and youth.* New York: Holt, Rinehart & Winston.

PUNISHMENT

Axelrod, S., Moyer, L., & Berry, B. C. (1983). *The effects of punishment on human behavior.* New York: Academic Press.

Clarizio, H. F. (1980). *Toward positive classroom discipline* (3rd ed.). New York: Wiley.

MacMillian, D. L., Forness, S. R., & Trumbull, B. M. (1973). The role of punishment in the classroom. *Exceptional Children, 40,* 85–97.

Rose, T. L. (1983). A survey of corporal punishment of mildly handicapped students. *Exceptional Education Quarterly, 3*, 9–19.

Wood, F. H., & Braaten, S. (1983). Developing guidelines for the use of punishing interventions in schools. *Exceptional Education Quarterly, 3*, 68–75.

EXCLUSION

Bartlett, L. (1989). Disciplining handicapped students: Legal issues in light of Honig v. Doe. *Exceptional Children, 55*, 357–366.

Craft, N., & Haussman, S. (1983). Suspension and expulsion of handicapped individuals. *Exceptional Children, 49*, 524–527.

Weckstein, P. (1982). *School discipline and student rights: An advocate's manual* (revised ed.). Cambridge, MA: Center for Law and Education.

Yell, M. L. (1989). Honig v. Doe: The suspension of handicapped students. *Exceptional Children, 56*, 60–69.

LEGAL ISSUES

Barton, L. E., Brulle, A. R., & Repp, A. C. (1983). Aversive techniques and the doctrine of least restrictive alternatives. *Exceptional Education Quarterly, 3*, 1–8.

Martin, R. (1975). *Legal challenges to behavior modification: Trends in schools, corrections, and mental health.* Champaign, IL: Research Press.

Weckstein, P. (1982). *School discipline and student rights: An advocate's manual* (revised ed.). Cambridge, MA: Center for Law and Education.

BEHAVIORAL EVALUATION

Alberto, P. A., & Troutman, A. C. (1990). *Applied behavior analysis for teachers: Influencing student performance.* Columbus, OH: Merrill.

Axelrod, S. (1983). *Behavior modification for the classroom teacher* (2nd ed.). New York: McGraw-Hill.

Cooper, J. O. (1981). *Measuring behavior* (2nd ed.). Columbus, OH: Merrill.

Craighead, W. E., Kazdin, A. E., & Mahoney, M. J. (1976). *Behavior modification: Principles, issues, and applications.* Boston: Houghton Mifflin.

Hersen, M., & Barlow, D. H. (1976). *Single-case experimental designs: Strategies for studying behavior change.* New York: Pergamon Press.

Johnson, J. M., & Pennypacker, H. S. (1980). *Strategies and tactics of human behavioral research.* Hillsdale, NJ: Erlbaum.

Martin, G., & Pear, J. (1978). *Behavior modification: What it is and how to do it.* Englewood Cliffs, NJ: Prentice-Hall.

SCHOOL VIOLENCE AND CRIME

Center, D. B., & McKittrick, S. (1987). Disciplinary removal of special education students. *Focus on Exceptional Children, 20*(2), 1–10.

Hranitz, J. R., & Eddowes, E. A. (1990). Violence: A crisis in homes and schools. *Childhood Education, 67*(1), 4–7.

Muir, E. (1990). *Report of the school safety department for the 1989–90 school year.* New York: United Federation of Teachers.

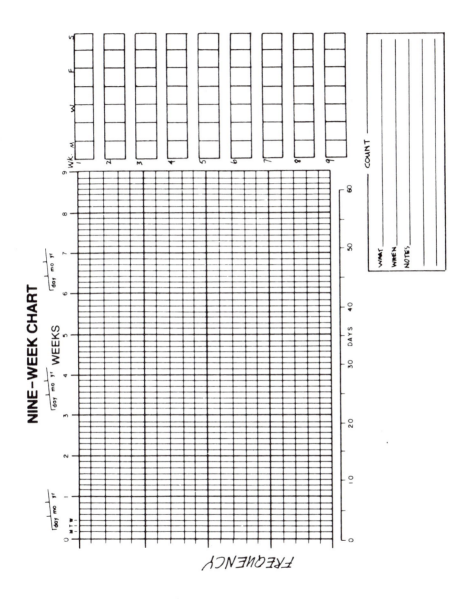

Subject Index